Can I Have
5 Minutes
of Your Time?

Can I Have
5 Minutes
of Your Time

By Hal Becker
with Florence Mustric

A no-nonsense, fun approach to sales
for all salespersons
from Xerox's former number one salesperson
in the U.S.A.

Oakhill Press
Akron & New York

Can I Have 5 Minutes of Your Time?

Library of Congress Cataloging-in-Publication Data

Becker, Hal B.
    Can I Have 5 Minutes of Your Time? / by Hal Becker
with Florence Mustric.

      ISBN 0-96195907-X (pb):$12.95
      1.Selling. 2. Sales personnel. I. Mustric, Florence.
II. Title: Can I Have 5 Minutes of Your Time?

HF5438.25.B4   1993
658.85--dc20
                             93-15399
                               CIP

12 13 14 15 16 17 18 19 20

To my late father and late mother, Joseph and Eunice, who taught me everything, including the principles I have always lived by. My only regret is that they are not here to share this moment which is the culmination of everything they gave me.

— Thank you!

Contents

Foreward . . . . **xiii**
How To Get More Dates

Acknowledgements . . . . **xv**

1. What It Takes to Be the Best **1**

Point 1. Desire and attitude are vital.
Point 2. All of us sell every day.
Point 3. "I'll never go back there again!"
Point 4. Picasso, Renoir, and Jones.
Point 5. The plumber's secret.
Point 6. The fable of the two woodsmen.
Point 7. How to be the cream of the crop.
Point 8. Think back (shudder!) to
          the last time you bought a car.
Point 9. 12:00! 12:00! 12:00!
Point 10. Do you sell confusion?
Point 11. Take the winning athlete's
          approach.
Point 12. What's new under the sun?
Point 13. All you need to know about
          human relations.

2. The Five Habits of a Top Salesperson **17**

Point 1. These five habits will set you
          apart from the pack.
Point 2. How to make resolutions
          that work.
Point 3. The secret of the top pros—
          in sales and sports.
Point 4. Working smarter is fine as long
          as you keep working harder.
Point 5. Make it fun!

3. Effective Listening is Essential for Effective Selling **29**

    Point 1. Favorable attitudes and listening.
    Point 2. How can you get customers to trust you?
    Point 3. How good a listener are you?
    Point 4. Spare-thinking time.
    Point 5. Tips to help make you a better listener.
    Point 6. Ask questions the way doctors do.
    Point 7. Your job is to investigate and to satisfy the customer.

4. Confidence: You Must Earn It. It's Worth It! . . . **39**

    Point 1. The benefits of confidence.
    Point 2. You have to earn it and you can.
    Point 3. How to make a positive impression.
    Point 4. Price is rarely the issue.
    Point 5. Testimonial: confidence sells.
    Point 6. High-impact workout to build self-confidence.
    Point 7. How bad can it get?

5. The Use of Questions in Selling **49**

    Point 1. The art and absolute importance of using questions.
    Point 2. It's not cheating. It's being prepared.
    Point 3. The art of conversation and your class reunion.
    Point 4. Questions give you the initiative.
    Point 5. Questions allow you to tune in to your customer's style and needs.
    Point 6. You have license to ask questions.
    Point 7. The trial close: the question that establishes commitment.

Point 8. How to use questions to probe for real wants and needs.

Point 9. The anatomy of a real live sales call in eight steps.

Point 10. The girl of my dreams.

Point 11. Another proof: the art of cross-examination.

Point 12. Simplify!

Point 13. Make Columbo your hero.

Point 14. Remember Dale Carnegie?

6. Overcoming Objections **73**

Point 1. How to understand and handle objections.

Point 2. Techniques that help you deal with objections.

Point 3. Gang up on objections.

Point 4. Why do you want objections? Consider these amazing facts.

Point 5. When the girl of my dreams says no.

7. Cold Call Selling **77**

Point 1. There are only two ways to get new business, and they aren't marketing and advertising.

Point 2. When you really want to dance.

Point 3. The truth about Babe Ruth.

Point 4. Which is better, in person or by phone?

Point 5. How many cold calls do you make each day? Consistency counts.

Point 6. Smarter, okay. Harder, yes!

Point 7. The screen.

Point 8. Screens were not born yesterday.

Point 9. Work while you wait.

Point 10. Your cold call is not a sales call

Point 11. You can learn a lot on 1,400 tours.
Point 12. When to take a rain check.
Point 13. How would you like to get
          six days of work done in five?
Point 14. Bob's secret.
Point 15. My favorite blizzard.
Point 16. How to use the telephone in
          cold calling.
Point 17. A great phone technique with
          the screen.
Point 18. Fax Becker.
Point 19. A strategy for under a buck for
          prospects who won't return
          your calls.
Point 20. Another technique that works and
          costs less than a buck.

8. Customer Care **101**
Point 1. To your customers, your company
          is you and everyone in it.
Point 2. Pray for problems.
Point 3. What to do when your contact
          keeps changing.
Point 4 It's 4:45 on a Friday afternoon.
Point 5. When customers don't know what
          they want.
Point 6 Take care of your customers: the
          satisfied ones and the dissatisfied
          ones.
Point 7. How to make your customer com-
          fortable with the decision to buy.
Point 8. Protect your reputation.
Point 9. "The Guy in the Glass."
Point 10. The dissatisfied customer.
Point 11. The nicest thing about the '90's.
Point 12. You have more dissatisfied cus-
          tomers than you realize!

Point 13. Smarter? No. Angrier? Yes!
Point 14. A week in the life of a customer.
Point 15. Reputation: it's all you've got.
Point 16. How about dessert? Add-on sales.

9. A Case in Point 119

Point 1. What does the customer want?
           Let's look again at the car dealer-
           ship on your corner.

10. Goal Setting and Time Management 123

Point 1. Goals: your rudder.
Point 2. Two ways to save time on
           proposals.
Point 3. Setting goals.
Point 4. Manage your time if you want
           to succeed.
Point 5. A $5 daily planner will change
           your life!
Point 6. How to plan your day.
Point 7. For a buck or so, you can get
           highly organized.
Point 8. Keep it all in perspective.

11. The Art of Closing 137

Point 1. When should you close?
Point 2. So you don't die.
Point 3. Do you think it's harder than
           it is?
Point 4. Symptoms of unnecessary fear
           of closing.
Point 5. Traits of a successful closer.
Point 6. Half the game is in watching.
Point 7. I took the manual off the shelf
           and made it a game.
Point 8. The order blank close.
Point 9. The alternative choice close.

Point 10. The free trial a.k.a. puppy close.

Point 11. The Ben Franklin close.

Point 12. The call back close.

Point 13. The lost sale close

Point 14. The "I'll think it over" close.

Point 15. The question close.

Point 16. The similar situation close.

Point 17. Develop flexibility and variety.

Point 18. From the buyer's side.

Point 19. Getting through the valleys.

Point 20. Why salespeople fail:
           David Sandler's four
           general assumptions.

Foreword

How to get more dates.

My search for dates landed me with the company that has the largest sales training program in the world: Xerox Corporation.

When I got out of college in 1976, my goal in life was to sell medical supplies. That's because a guy who's 21 years old thinks with one thing: testosterone. My brain said: medical supplies... nurses... dates.

I couldn't get a job selling medical supplies. Some guys who lived in my apartment building worked for Xerox, and they said, "Why don't you come work for Xerox?" I told them, "I don't want to sell copiers. I want to sell medical supplies." That was in May. In September my money was running out, so I decided to go for a job at Xerox. After six or seven interviews, I got hired.

I thought to myself, "This is not a bad company. They have about 11,000 salespeople and a great sales training program. I'll stay here one year, get this great training, make myself marketable—and then I'll go sell medical supplies."

The training was unbelievable. The sessions ran three weeks at a time, 12-14 hours a day—and night. Xerox spent millions of dollars developing and improving on all these sales tools they had picked up from everyone else.

The first year I did pretty well. I was in the top 20% of our branch. I thought, "I'll apply all this information. I'll take the stuff they're telling me and just work harder than the next guy." In my second year at Xerox, in 1977, I was number one in the entire U.S. I thought, "Wow! I think I'll stay awhile...."

I am not an exception. In 1983 Xerox did a study of its 500 top salespeople and found that:

> Diligent application makes the difference between an average salesperson and a successful salesperson.

It's all in the application of skills. I did it. And so can you.

In this book, I talk a lot about dating and buying a car because they are experiences we can all relate to. If I break sales down into common-sense things we all do, you can more readily apply them to selling.

Every day I work with people who are new to sales and have never sold before. I also work with people who have been selling for years, except THEY've never sold either—because most salespeople don't do it right.

Acknowledgements

Many People helped me with *Can I Have 5 Minutes of Your Time?* One thing is for sure, I could never have done this project alone.

First off, my special thanks goes to Florence Mustric, whose genius and creativity enabled me to put my seminars in book form. She transformed words into mental pictures, and molded serious selling techniques with her wonderful sense of humor which made this book *fun* to read.

All the people at Oakhill Press were the best. Roger Herman for being the deal maker, and *never* going back on anything he said. Jim Bartlett and Trudy Dheel for overseeing this project from start to finish, and keeping everything on schedule. Bob Wilkey, the photographer, for his unique style of shooting the cover, and not yelling at me once. Also, we cannot forget Estelle Herman, our editor, for proofing all my stupid third grade mistakes, and Denis Lange, the greatest art director in Ashland, Ohio.

Bob Shook provided his keen wisdom and book publishing expertise throughout the four years when we began this project. I am grateful for his help, generosity of his time, and above all, his belief in me as a first-time author.

Lastly, all my close friends who are still in shock that I was able to even read a book, let alone write one, and to Jon Lief, who's creative warped mind came up with the title of this book in 27 seconds.

Ten steps to getting the most out of this book—and out of life!

1. As you read, stop at the end of every page or section and ask yourself, "How can I apply this to my situation?"
2. Mark each important idea.
3. Read each chapter twice before going to the next one.
4. Remind yourself that you can and will succeed in sales—and every other endeavor—by building positive habits.
5. Use the ideas and principles in this book every day, in every situation.
6. Review your progress at the end of every day. What did you do better? Where can you improve?
7. Review this book every month.
8. Make a game out of building good habits. Reward yourself for every success. Start a contest with co-workers or with friends.
9. Look for new ideas and examples around you.
10. Enjoy!

Can I Have
5 Minutes
of Your Time?

1

What It takes to Be the Best

Point 1. Desire and attitude are vital.

It takes time. Whenever we start something new, it's uncomfortable. What was it like riding a bike the first time? When you first diapered your baby, were you scared? What about your first lesson in learning a foreign language? The key is practice. And most salespeople don't practice.

To practice is to be in training. I can train people to sell, but there's just one catch. You have to *want* to learn, to practice, to excel. *I can't* train *desire.* And without the desire, there isn't a ghost of a chance of training anyone.

Attitude is vital. Truth is, if you have a great attitude, it's so easy to be the best. So often when we go out to buy, to eat, to do whatever, we get bad service. I'm sure that if you think about what happens day in and day out, you will realize that almost every day you have an experience that's bad or leaves a lot to be desired. We'll discuss that later.

It's *easy* to be the best. All you have to do is to have a better attitude and be a little better than everyone else.

This piece by Charles Swindoll says it all about attitude.

Attitude

The longer I live, the more I realize the impact of attitude on life. Attitude is more important than facts. It is more important than the past, than circumstances, than money, than education, than failures or successes, or what other people think or say or do. It's more important than appearance, giftedness, or skill. We cannot change our past. We cannot change the fact that people act in a certain way. We have no control over the inevitable. The only thing we can do is pull on the one string we have, and that is our attitude.

The remarkable thing is that we have a choice every day regarding the attitude we embrace for that day. I am convinced that life is 10% what actually happens to me and 90% how I react to it.

So it is with you. We are all in charge of our own attitudes.

Point 2. Whether or not you're in sales, you sell every day.

If I could ask you right now whether you are in sales, the chances are only 50-50 that you would say yes. You might say no: you're in accounting or technical or maybe you're the owner. Regardless of your answer, this book can help you.

If you are in sales, we're discussing the lifeblood of your livelihood and your contribution to your company.

And if you are *not* in sales, you will still find ideas and tools that will help you do your job or run your business more profitably. And the topics that don't apply to you directly, such as prospecting, will still be informative and useful.

The ideas and tools of sales are useful in accounting, marketing, shipping, *any*thing. Whatever your job or business, if you deal with a customer or client in *any* way, you are selling.

That's why some business owners and managers have their entire company or division attend sales seminars.

The truth is that all of us are selling every day:

We're selling a product or service.

We're selling our company.

We're selling our ideas, ourselves.

Point 3. "I'll never go back there again!"

Your reputation rides on what you do and say today.

Have you ever been to a restaurant and had really poor service? Where the waiter or waitress was so bad you couldn't believe it? What do you do? Do you ever go back? Not if you can help it! And what do you tell people? "Don't go there! It's a terrible restaurant!"

But in essence it wasn't the restaurant that was bad— it was that one person who was bad or just having a bad day.

And where your company's customer has a bad experience in accounting, in technical support, in shipping, what does your customer say to people in other companies? "Don't use so-and-so. They're not so hot."

We're constantly selling. And I'll be constantly telling you that as I discuss all the aspects of selling: how to listen, how to build your confidence, how to ask questions and to probe, how to handle objections, how to go out and get the business, how to close the sale, and—most important, no matter what you do, how to *keep* the business!

Point 4. Picasso, Renoir, and Jones.

Let's talk fo. a moment about art forms. Cleveland,

my home town, has one of the most magnificent art museums *any*where. You can see some of the greatest— and most beautiful—artistry at the Cleveland Museum of Art: masterpieces by Renoir, Monet, Picasso.

These three of the world's greatest artists all share three things in common: paint, brushes, and canvas. But yet their works are completely different. Why? because of the creativity and uniqueness of the artist.

The same thing is true of all of us. You can't expect to be like me or the next person.

You have to use your own creativity, what's inside you, along with the basic tools I'll be giving you in the course of this book—the paint, brushes, and canvas of the art of selling.

You have your good points. I don't care what your situation is: how much experience you have, what you're selling, or what your personality is. You have good points, and they work well for you. Build on those good points, and develop your style around them. You can become the Picasso of sales.

Point 5. The plumber's secret.

Did you ever change a faucet at home? And did you try to do it with whatever tool you had around, or did you use a special tool—like a ratchet—that goes under the sink?

If you didn't use the right tool, what was it like? It was hell! And how long did it take? Forever! But if you have the *right* tool, the job takes only a few minutes, and it's a snap!

So it's the tool that makes the difference. All I'm doing is providing you with the tools. It's up to you to put your style into selling—to become a Picasso.

This book is a tool. It's based on my seminar and manual, also a tool. Out of every 100 people I work with, only five people will really, diligently, use this tool to change their lives.

Above all, you must have the desire. You must want to make the effort it takes to make things happen.

Point 6. The fable of the two woodsmen.

I don't usually like sales trainer stories, but this one just blew me away.

Two woodsmen had a contest to see who could chop the most wood on a given day. One guy's big, 270 pounds, and the other small, or as they say, "the Hal Becker size." The big guy looks at the small guy and thinks, "There's no way this guy can beat me."

The contest lasts eight hours. Every 45 minutes the small guy takes a break. He just leaves and goes off somewhere. The big guy thinks, "Yep, there's no way that small guy is going to beat me."

When they chop the wood, it's put in separate areas. At the end of the day, the piles are measured. Guess what? The small guy has chopped twice as much wood as the big guy.

The big guy is furious. He can't believe it. He says to the small guy, "I don't understand. First, I'm twice your size and twice your strength, and you've chopped twice as much wood. On top of that, every 45 minutes you rolled off and took a break, a nap—I don't know what you did. How did you cheat me and beat me?"

The small guy says, "I didn't cheat. It was easy to beat you because every 45 minutes, when you thought I was taking a break, I was out back sharpening my ax."

That's what we're talking about: sharpening your ax.

Most salespeople do such a poor job because they don't go back to the basics. They don't go back to their common-sense tools—the tools I'm going to give you. They didn't *sharpen* their *skills*.

Point 7. How to be the cream of the crop.

Three things make the top salesperson. This applies to *you* whether you are 100% in sales or not, whatever your title.
- Top sales people are **organized**
- Top salespeople are **persistent.**

And, most important:
- Top salespeople are **incredibly honest.**

What exactly is selling?

I'm going to give you a definition of selling. It's this book in a nutshell.

Before you look up selling in a dictionary, let me save you the trouble. You'll find at least a dozen definitions, but I guarantee you won't find the *real* definition of selling.

Selling is asking, *not* telling.

Selling is listening, *not* talking.

Those ten words are so important that I'm going to repeat them:

> *Selling is asking, NOT telling.*
> *Selling is listening, NOT talking.*

Everything I tell you will be built around these ten words to show you what it takes to be a top salesperson.

The truth is—and it's a shame—that most salespeople do a terrible job.

They are not organized.

They are not persistent.

They are not incredibly honest.

Worst of all, they do not ask. And they do not listen.

Point 8. Think back (shudder!) to the last time you bought a car.

Chances are your family bought a car in the past year. And I'll bet it was an unpleasant experience. On the whole, car salespeople—new cars and used—have a terrible reputation. The responsibility, I think, rests with the sales manager—instead of coaching the sales force, the manager's making all those deals.

When you walk in, the salespeople just hang around. They try to push features you don't want. They don't know their product—ask at five dealerships how many gallons the gas tank holds, and you'll get five different answers.

And when you finally get down to dealing on a car, the salesperson has to get involved with the manager—assuming there IS a manager. Can't you just imagine what goes on in back? One salesperson says to another, "Hey, Greg! You wannabe the manager today?" Of course you want to pay a good price.

When you asked the salesperson, "What's my price?" then you have to go back and forth and deal, deal, deal. Another unpleasant experience. Have you ever gotten the top salesperson or the owner? It's a real pleasant experience—real different, isn't it?

Car salespeople are also remarkably poor on customer service. Consider this amazing fact: the average U.S. family buys one car a year, a statistic which makes sense when you realize that two out of three cars sold are used cars.

That statistic represents a wonderful opportunity to develop a relationship with a customer who is going to be buying again—soon! It also should represent a very potent motivator, when you consider the fact that dealers spend an average of $250 on advertising for everybody who walks in the door.

And car salespeople are also remarkably poor on customer service if you consider that car manufacturers have a Customer Satisfaction Index which requires something probably unique in sales: the salesperson must call the buyer after the sale.

Volkswagen developed the Customer Service Index in 1978 to see how the dealers stacked up against each other. One of the requirements is that the salesperson must follow up with you after delivery—with a minimum of two phone calls the first year of ownership, regardless of what make of car you buy.

The manufacturer in effect says, "We need to know if the dealers are really doing their jobs. We'll do this by sending out a survey to the buyers to find out if they're satisfied." A dealer who gets great survey results can get more cars, a better mix of cars, more promotional materials, and so on.

You may not realize it, but every dealership in the country pays the exact same amount for any given car. The salespeople create the imbalance and the competition.

Despite this rule, many salespeople do not make even one call. Often they're afraid the owner might have a problem. (The possibility of a problem should actually motivate them to call—I walk around looking for problems, because a problem is a *creative opportunity* for me to be a hero.)

Many car salespeople do make one follow-up call. But I'll bet that you did not get more than one call. And if you got more than two phone calls, it means that salesperson cares and wants to sell you more cars. If you did get more than two calls, would you buy another car from this salesperson?

Point 9. 12:00! 12:00! 12:00! Another disaster area—or a golden opportunity?

Where else does the selling-and-buying experience leave something to be desired? Let's step inside the homes of thousands of Americans, where right this minute the VCR is blinking 12:00! 12:00! 12:00!

What happened when you bought a VCR? You probably walked into a store thinking, "I want to tape television shows and rent movies." The salesman tells you, "We've got three machines. This here is our Azmuth-Head, and here is our 4-Head-Fly-Erasing Machine, and over here is our VCR with the Dylethium crystals."

All this leaves you more confused than when you walked in. All the VCR's look the same to you, so what do you do? You end up buying on price, and you get out of there.

Ahh! Home at last! You plug the VCR in, then you look at the instruction manual, which pretends to be written in English. So you throw down the manual, and you play around with the buttons for about half an hour.

If you're like most of us, you get as far as 12:00! 12:00! 12:00! At this point you have two choices: translate the manual into understandable English or find a 6-year-old who can do it.

I suggest you find a 6-year-old.

Let's replay that scenario. You want to buy a VCR, and you walk into Hal's VCR World. Hal walks up to help you....

Hal: "...before I show you a few VCR's, let me ask you a few questions. First of all, how much did you plan to spend?"

Sue: "Oh, about $250."

Hal: "Do you want a VCR to rent movies and tape television shows?"

Sue: "That's it.

Hal: "Okay, wireless remote is obviously important, and it's standard on all these models. Do you ever travel for more than two weeks at a time?"

Sue: "No."

Hal:"Do you have a stereo in the same room as your television set?"

Sue: "Yes."

Hal: "And when you go to the theater and hear Dolby Hi-Fi Surround Sound—would you like to have it at home?"

Sue: "That would be great!"

Hal: "Do you like sporting events?"

Sue: "No."

Hal: "So slow motion and special effects, like watching the threads on the football go by real slowly, aren't important to you?"

Sue: "Right."

Hal: "In that case, I'd recommend one of two machines. Both are wireless remote, and both tape two weeks at a time, so you have 14 days of taping available. The first machine, which is high quality, or HQ, is $197. For another $100, or $297, you can have the same machine plus Dolby Hi-Fi stereo so you can have that theater sound in your family room. Which do you prefer?"

Sue: "I want the one with the Dolby!"

What just happened? Did Sue walk out with what she planned to buy or what she planned to spend? No.

But did she walk out with what she wanted? Yes!

But when she goes home, takes the VCR out of the box, and tries to set it up, she's probably still going to get a bit confused. Let's go to the next day in our scenario. The phone rings.

Hal: "Hi, Sue? This is Hal from Hal's VCR World. How's the VCR?"

Sue: "Great." [93% of new VCR owners say that, but they don't mean it!]

Hal: "Have you figured out yet how to work the clock and the timer?"

Sue: "No."

Hal: "When you have 10 minutes, I'll walk you through the process of setting the clock and the timer."

Sue: "That would be great!"

Hal: "We can do it now if you have time."

Is Sue going to be impressed? Yes. Will she tell other people? You bet she will! During the course of the year, I call her another two or three times:

Hal: "Hi, Sue? This is Hal from Hal's VCR World. I just called to say hi. How's the VCR?"

Is she really, *really* going to be impressed? Selling VCR's or cars is no different from anything else. It's just that we all experience first-hand the frustrations of buying VCR's and cars.

What did I do with Sue? I found out what was important. I didn't bombard her with technical talk. I didn't confuse her or let her stay confused.

And I followed up. It's the same whatever you're selling.

Point 10. Do you sell confusion? Most salespeople sell confusion. And customers hate it!

If you've ever been around business owners when

they got their first computer, you know how scared they were to take their business and put it on computer. That's because most computer companies don't make the product and the transition easy.

A corporation is...

A corporation is just a piece of paper. Anyone can have a corporation for a couple hundred bucks. Companies are people, and the better those people work together as a team, the healthier that company will be. If someone in sales needs something from someone in service, it's not a matter of cadging a favor. It's a matter of everyone working together.

A good company is people who care. The style of successful companies can be anything from conservative to crazy, but at every successful company everyone works together to get the job done.

For managers and owners, it all comes down to one thing called MBWA: Management By Walking Around. Tom Peters made a fortune consulting on those four words. Finding out what the customers want. The only way you're going to be successful is to find out what your customers want...because guess what you don't have if you don't have customers?

Without customers, you don't have a job.

Without customers, you don't have a company.

Your customers are the ones who make you healthy. A winning company is people who care passionately all the time.

Point 11. Take the winning athlete's approach.

Vince Lombardi, coach of the Green Bay Packers

back in the 1970's, said it all: Winning is not a some-time thing.

You don't win once in a while.

You don't do things right once in a while.

You do them right all the time.

That's the key—doing things right *all* the time. That comes down to attitude. We'll look at attitude later and at ways to build a great attitude.

Point 12. What's new under the sun?

What's new about these tools? If you looked in the front of my book, you'd see that it says *copyright*. What that really means is *plagiarized*.

I have nothing new. All this information was taken from Xerox, Procter & Gamble, Kodak, IBM, Leaseway, and a number of other companies. They all took *their* stuff from other companies. There is nothing new in sales training. If you read Dale Carnegie's book, which is over 60 years old, you'll find it all there.

Look at Tom Peters, who wrote *In Search of Excellence, Thriving on Chaos,* and *A Passion for Excellence.* He gets $20,000 (or more) to run a seminar. He's unbelievable to listen to. He's a ball of energy. What is he selling? He sells things we already know: common sense. He packages common sense with enthusiasm. He sells enthusiasm.

You won't learn anything new from me, unless you've never taken a sales course. More likely, you'll say, "Oh yeah, I forgot to do that."

People buy from people.

That's my theme. Your products and services are sec-ondary. People don't ask, "Where you are located? What's your building like? How many square feet do you have?"

Do you, the customer, really care about whether you're buying a SuperScanner or a Hitachi monitor or an MGA monitor? Does it make a difference? *No.*

Does it really matter whether the processor on your computer is a 486 Intel or a Motorola? Again, *no.*

What makes a difference is *you.*

If you have the lowest price in the world but you're nasty, what will your customers do? They'll go to your competitors. People buy from people. If you can't stand the people at the car dealership on your corner, you'll buy your car somewhere else.

Point 13. All you need to know: a short course in human relations.

It seems that everyone but me has always known that Dear Abby and Ann Landers are twin sisters. These two women, more than everyone else put together, tell us how to do things right in our lives.

Among the pearls of wisdom you can find in their column (and elsewhere) are The Most Important Words in the English Language. You may already be familiar with these words. Let's take a few moments to review them, because in the course of this book we'll be thinking about them in the context of sales.

The six most important words:

"I was wrong. Please forgive me."

Let's say I'm the new boss and I tell you to do things one way. Then I realize I was wrong. I say:

"I appreciate that you listened to what I said, but I was wrong...."

What would you think? I'm a straight shooter. I'm not just thinking about myself.

The five most important words:

"You did a good job."

You're new on the job and I tell you:

"You did a pretty good job doing what we asked you to do today. In fact, you did it better than the last person."

How do you feel about yourself? You feel good!

The four most important words:

"What is your opinion?"

That shows I value what you think and want to take it into consideration.

The three most important words:

"Can I help?"

You have a flat tire on the freeway, and I stop to help you. I don't steal your money or attack you. All I do is help you fix your tire, and I'm on my way. You think, "There's at least one good guy left out there."

The two most important words:

"Thank you."

The one most important word:

"You."

The least important word:

"I."

If you find yourself in a sales conversation where you are saying, "I can do this, and I can do that, and I...." then it's insincere.

Here's the difference between "I" and "you":

Phil has just met Michelle at a party. He asks her, "Where are you from? Where do you work? What do you do there? Where do you live? Tell me about your family."

When he leaves, I say to Michelle, "I see you've been talking to Phil. What's he like?" Michelle says, "He's a great guy." If I ask her, "Oh yeah? Where does he live?

What does he do?" Michelle doesn't know. She likes him because he took an interest in her and because she was talking.

In one of my seminars, when I asked, "Why does Michelle like Phil?" a woman said, "She likes him *because* she doesn't know anything about him!"

When you have the opportunity to talk about yourself, you like the person you're talking to.

> ***So when you're in a sales situation, get the customer to talk.***

2

The Five Habits of a Top Salesperson.

Point 1. These five habits will set you apart from the pack.

These habits for success were determined by Xerox a few years back. Observers analyzed 500 sales calls made by people selling a variety of products and services. Xerox found that the top salespeople, regardless of their product or service, consistently used five techniques.

Make a habit of these five techniques. They work for everyone. They will work for you. Let me sum them up very quickly.

The Five Habits of Top Salespeople.

Habit 1. Successful salespeople spend more time asking questions and listening than they spend talking.

Habit 2. Successful salespeople translate features into benefits.

Habit 3. Successful salespeople probe for more information instead of jumping to conclusions.

Habit 4. Successful salespeople address negative customer attitudes—objections, indifference, and skepticism—promptly and directly.

Habit 5. Successful salespeople identify closing signals and act upon them immediately.

These are skills and habits anyone can learn. If you

apply these skills and make them a part of yourself, then you will be successful. You will become one of the few.

I mentioned this in the introduction, but it's so important it bears repeating. Xerox summed up its study this way:

> Diligent application of selling skills can make the difference between an average salesperson and a successful salesperson.

From my own experience, I see how this works. On a typical day, 100-200 people attend my seminar. They all receive the same manual. They all hear me say the same things. A couple of these people will dig in and really apply the material. A couple of them will do nothing—they are just going through the motions. Everyone else is in the middle: they say, "I'll get around to it tomorrow."

Point 2. How to make resolutions that work.

It's the same with any resolution. How often have YOU tried to lose weight, work out, or quit smoking? I belong to a health club, and the one time I hate it is in January. I call January the Resolutionists' month. The place is crowded with everyone who made a New Year's resolution to shape up. By the middle of February, they've given up, and the club is back to normal.

If you want an unbelievable body, you have to work out. If you exercise eight hours today and then do nothing until next September, nothing will happen. But if you do a little bit four times a week, you're not going to burn yourself out. You'll have dramatic results in three to six months.

Whatever you want you can do, but you have to want it badly enough. The same is true in sales, business—anything. You've got to make it happen.

Habit #1: Listen!

Listening is a real art. I'll discuss it in depth later, but for now let me say this:

Xerox found that listening is at least as important as talking. Successful salespeople begin their presentation by asking questions to gather information and uncover customer needs. This not only helps the salesperson tailor his or her talk to what the customer is really interested in, but it also gets the buyer actively involved in the presentation.

Equally important, successful salespeople ask questions which can*not* be answered simply yes or no; yes-no answers give the customer little opportunity to talk.

Habit #2: Features never sold a thing.

A feature is what the product does; features don't sell anything. A benefit is what's in it for the customer; benefits are what sell customers.

Successful salespeople talk about how their product or service can satisfy customer needs. This has become a truism of sales, but a surprising number of salespeople fail to apply this technique consistently. And, believe it or not, many salespeople have trouble distinguishing features from benefits.

By comparison, television commercials are very good at focusing on benefits. For example, the mouthwash Scope has an ingredient called T2-3: that's a *feature* of the product, and the commercials don't spend a lot of time talking about T2-3. They do focus on what T2-3 does, on what the *benefit* is for the customer: Scope keeps your breath minty fresh: that's the benefit.

Strangely enough, we have no trouble identifying benefits when we are *buy*ing; it's just when we're selling that we somehow get so involved in our own process and product that we don't focus on the customer in front of us—we don't ask ourselves, "What does this human being really want?"

Back to your car. What brand of air-conditioning compressor do you have? You don't care. You just want your car to keep you cool, even when you put the pedal to the metal to pass a truck.

Every time you think of a company feature, follow through with *the benefit: what's in it for the customer.* That's all your customer cares about!

Habit #3: Probing, or How Joe Found True Love.

Xerox found that probing makes a vital difference. Let's return to the world of dating to see the difference between the person who probes and the person who doesn't.

Here's just-average Bo, who ignores probing entirely:

Bo: "Hey, Sue, let's go out for a cup of coffee."

Sue: "No."

Bo: "(to himself) Darn!"

Now here's successful Joe, who uses probing effectively:

Joe: "Hey, Sue, how about going out for a cup of coffee?"

Sue: "No."

Joe: "Can I ask you one more question?"

Sue: "Sure."

Joe: *"Why not?"*

Sue: "I don't think you're interesting." (translation: "You're pond scum. Get outta my face!")

Sue *could* have said, "I'm busy. I have to do laundry tonight. Ask me again!" But Joe has to find out why she said no.

All of us who have been single have been dumped on at one time or another. At that point, you have two choices.

You can think:

"I'm depressed. I'm going to stay home and knit a car."

Or you can say to yourself:

"I'm going to make it happen. I'm going to call some friends and go on blind dates. I'll go to health clubs, singles bars, and singles night at the local supermarket."

If you go out on one blind date, what are the chances of meeting someone you really like? Zip, probably. But if you go out on *ten* blind dates, just twenty minutes for coffee, do you have a better chance of meeting someone? Absolutely!

What's the difference? It's a numbers game. The more numbers, the better your chances.

On a show called "Love Connection," a guest said he dates twenty times a month. Twenty! Doesn't he have a job? With twenty blind dates, he sure has a much better chance of meeting someone.

Back to Sue and Joe. When you get a *no,* all you want to do is to find the answer to one question:

"Why not?"

Joe: "Sue, let me ask you some questions. What do you like to do?"

Sue: "I like to go to Club Coconuts every night and dance until four in the morning."

If Joe's a homebody and she wants to dance every night, is this a match made in heaven? No! But if Joe likes to go to Club Coconuts too, then he and Sue have some similar interests. Now it's Joe's job to get Sue to trust him and then, if possible, to like him. Isn't that what makes a relationship work?

Show me something different in selling. It's really the same thing. You have to find out what the customer wants and if you can give it to him. Then your job is to get the customer to trust you. If he or she likes you, that's a bonus.

Xerox found that probing follow-up questions, often overlooked by mediocre salespeople, provide pay-dirt. For example: a customer complained that his existing equipment wasn't fast enough. I asked how important speed really was. It turned out that speed was secondary to accuracy. This fact enabled me to focus on the benefit of accuracy in discussing equipment capability.

Selling is an investigative process. And it's all about dealing with people.

You're not selling computers or plastics or anything else. You *are* selling to people.

Most salespeople stink because they go out and sell what's best for *them* or try to push people into buying things they don't want or need. That is *not* selling.

Selling is an art form. Selling is not achieved through slick talking. It is achieved only through asking a series of questions.

Habit #4: Address the negatives.

Xerox found that successful salespeople address negative customer attitudes. Superior salespeople do *not* ignore any customer statements or body language indicating indifference, skepticism, or objections. The successful salesperson deals with such negative attitudes directly and promptly.

If you're talking to a customer and the customer isn't

saying anything, guess what: you ain't selling anything! But when a customer objects:

"That's more than I want to spend",
what that customer is really saying is,

"I'm interested, but you haven't found my price yet".

You're looking for the key that will unlock the door to the sale. And that key is an objection. Back to Joe and Sue:

Joe: "Why don't you want to go out?"

Sue: "I don't find you interesting."

Joe: "If I were more interesting to you, would you want to go out?"

Sue: "The answer is still no."

Guess what. Sue really *isn't* interested. But eventually Joe will find someone who *is*.

Habit #5: A strong close is critical.

Finally, Xerox found that a strong close is critical. As soon as true professionals identify a closing signal— even one as subtle as leaning back in a chair, they act immediately upon that signal and move to close the sale. They also realize that such a signal can occur at any time, even early in the call.

The most successful closing technique found in Xerox's study was this: a summary of benefits accepted by the customer and a plan requiring customer commitment, such as agreement to specific payment terms or a trial order. More about closing later.

The bottom line of this whole study *and* of careful reading of the expert literature is this:

There are no real secrets to successful selling. The only secret, it seems, is how to get salespeople to apply these well-known and proven techniques on a consistent basis!

It's just like working out. If you work out a little every day, consistently, you'll see results. Most salespeople don't know how to do this, or else they don't appreciate how much it will benefit them.

Keep in mind that with sales, as with anything, it takes time to get results. When you start building a new habit, it's uncomfortable, so be patient with yourself and persist until you reach a comfort level. If you're a parent, think back to the first time you changed a diaper. Weren't you scared? But soon you could almost do it in your sleep!

Do you remember your first kiss? Are you better now?

It's the same when you try to do anything new or when you have a new product or a new company. It's always uncomfortable. The key is practice, and most salespeople don't practice!

Point 3. The secret of the top pros—in sales and in sports—is consistency and practice.

A good coach and a good team.

I believe a good company is like a good coach with a good team. A team can't be good unless it has a good coach. What is a coach's job? The first job is to go out and find the best talent, and that means finding people who not only play well but who also have the best attitude: people who care. And the coach's second job is to see that those players practice—that they work their hearts out so that they maximize their potential.

Why do I say attitude is so important? Let me take a moment to talk about my dog. In two months I trained him to do what I wanted him to do. Eventually I could say one word, and that dog would listen to me and *do* what I wanted him to do.

If I can train a dog—an animal that doesn't under-stand English—to be a great pet, why can't I train every human being I work with to be a great salesperson?

The reason: to be a great salesperson, a human being must first have the desire. But most human beings don't have the desire, and *nobody* can train or teach desire. Without desire, I don't have a prayer of a chance to teach *any*one.

Look at professional sports and you'll find some of the best examples of consistency and practice in profes-sional sports. Look at the top golfers on the PGA tour or the basketball players who are the best foul shooters in the NBA.

Gary Player, one of the best golfers ever, is 5'6" and weighs about 135 pounds—and shoots in the 60's. Larry Bird is basketball's best foul shooter. What do you see them do before a match or a game? These top players practice. They have been playing for years, they're the best in the field, and they never stop practicing. That's how they stay at the top.

So why don't salespeople practice?

The N.B.A. star who's five feet tall.

Only in my dreams! It's true that for many sports you have to be born with certain qualities. But in sales, I guarantee you can be a star if you really want to. You don't need to be so tall or have a high I.Q. You just need to have the desire and have the tools to achieve your goal. Let me prove it two ways.

Point 4. Working smarter is fine as long as you keep working harder. Give it all you've got!

If you watch television late Sunday nights, you've

probably seen Herbalife's infomercial. In the audience are 4,000 or 5,000 people, all of whom sell Herbalife products. The leader starts by asking, "How many people have sold $10,000?" The entire audience is on its feet. When he asks, "How many people have sold more than $200,000?" ten or twelve people are still on their feet, and he calls them to the podium. The dialogue goes like this:

Leader: "How long have you been selling Herbalife?"

Seller: "Waall now, let me see, two years, give or take a couple months."

Leader: "And what did you do before that?"

Seller: "I herded sheep in Utah."

All the people in that audience bought the same sales kit for about $35. They all started on their friends and relatives. How did this ex-sheepherder do so well? He's just seeing more people and working harder.

Let me prove it one more way. In Cleveland and its suburbs, some 9,000 people have a real-estate license, but only 40 or 50 make the list as top salespeople, and only one is always at the top. These people are making serious money because they take real estate seriously. They work full-time at it, they've paid their dues over a period of years, and they work hard.

Point 5. One more thing: Make it fun. Enjoy yourself.

Approach selling as something that's fun. First of all, you want to enjoy your work. As I mentioned earlier, work should not feel like work. Of course we have to do certain things we don't want to do, but there are ways to make those things fun.

Second, we enjoy doing things we do well. Life is a

game. The better we play it, the more fun we have, and the more we get out of life. You'll enjoy the people around you more, and they'll enjoy you.

3

Effective Listening is Essential for Effective Selling

If you listen, *really* listen, you will be miles ahead of 99% of the rest of the world. And good listening is essential if you want to be good at selling.

Point 1. Favorable attitudes and listening.

Favorable attitudes affect listening.

You can easily reduce the way emotions affect a sales situation. Naturally, you prefer customers who agree with you. Such a prejudicial attitude causes them to selectively hear the positive content of your message. If a customer is not favorable to you, however, you must consider that he or she is not hearing all you are saying. As a matter of fact, such a customer is most probably formulating objections rather than listening closely.

Detect the unstated need.

Seldom do prospects identify their needs directly. Often a prospect will be unaware that you can positively affect his or her operation. Only by listening for the unstated clues will you be able to hear a customer's

needs and so find an opportunity to meet those needs
by selling your products or services.

Don't expect a listener to convey your message.

It's important to make all your sales presentations
personally. Don't let a company contact pass along the
message for you. It takes only one bad listener for communication to fail.

By listening well, you build trust.

Why do customers ask technical support people lots of
questions, instead of asking salespeople? They don't trust
salespeople—because most salespeople are so poor. But *if*
you are a *good* salesperson, the customer will trust you.

Point 2. How can you get customers to trust you?

In almost every seminar I have people who are in
technical support, accounting—an area *other* than sales.

I ask these non-salespersons:

"How many salespersons do you see in a typical
month?"

The average number is 10 or 12. Then I ask:

"Of the salespersons you see, how many are so
incredibly good that if they changed companies and
sold a different product or service, you would buy it
from them?"

The usual answer: they saw only one salesperson that
good—maybe none. Here's a typical comment from
someone not in sales:

"I don't like salespeople because I feel they're always
trying to manipulate me. They don't realize people can
see right through them. Salespeople make me feel so

uncomfortable. They should be real and honest, not put on a front."

Yet it's so *easy* to be *good if* you have the right attitude.

Remember our definition of sales?

Selling is listening, not talking.

Selling is asking, not telling.

By the way, do not say to a customer, "Let me be honest with you." That implies you have been lying up to that point.

> *Did you ever talk yourself out of a sale?*
> *Did you go on and on until it was too late?*
> *Did you ever LISTEN yourself out of a sale? Impossible!*

Point 3. How good a listener are you? Here are five questions.

You are in conversation with a customer. He's talking, and you interrupt. Give yourself two points.

A customer is talking. Instead of listening, you start thinking about what you're going to say. Two points.

A customer is talking... real slow... and it's... driving... you... cra... zy. You finish his sentence for him. Two points.

The customer is talking. You missed something or don't understand it. You don't ask to have it repeated or explained. Two points.

You've just been introduced to someone new. One minute later you realize you don't know her name. Two points!

If you scored 6 points or higher, you drastically need to improve your listening skills!

Failing to listen: it happens all the time in real life.

You're driving and you get lost, so you go into a gas station and ask, "Excuse me, Goober, how do I get to Nobottom Road?" He says, "Well, what you do is you go out the driveway, take a left, go down the road a piece, take a left at the first stop sign, and go over the railroad tracks. Veer to the right at the second traffic light, go around the bend, and you're there." You say, "Got it! Thanks." You get to the driveway, and you can't remember the first thing he said.

This is where we encounter the most basic difference between men and women. We men will not go back and ask for directions a second time (it was bad enough asking for them the *first* time!) because we're too proud. Don't let pride stand in the way of success.

**Why you have trouble remembering names—
and how to fix it.**

Have you ever met someone one moment and forgotten his or her name the next instant? Why do you do this? You're too busy sizing them up, concentrating on what they wear or what you're going to say or do. You're not listening. Try repeating the name. What happens now? When you hear yourself say the name, you remember it, particularly if you use the name a few more times, naturally, during that conversation.

Most people's minds work faster than their mouths. Unfortunately, most salespeople's mouths work faster than their minds. That's because they're always talking and never listening.

> *The most important aspect of your job is to understand what customers are really telling you. To do this, you have to listen more effectively.*

Point 4. Spare-thinking time.

We normally think a great deal faster than we speak. This gap gives you spare-thinking time in conversations. One of the most important ways to listen more effectively is to learn to put spare-thinking time to good use.

These five mental activities will help you attend to all that is being said:

1. Try to **anticipate** the direction the speaker is taking and the conclusions the speaker will make.
2. Determine whether the speaker is giving valid and complete **support** for the point he or she is making.
3. Periodically, mentally **summarize** the points made so far. Summarize ideas and concepts, not facts.
4. Concentrate on the **ideas** the speaker is trying to convey, not on the individual facts which support the ideas.
5. Attend to **nonverbal cues.** Search for meaning beyond the spoken words—that is, listen between the lines.

What would you do?

Let me paint the scene: You're finally in a prospect's office, making your presentation. Your prospect:

has his arms folded and his head down,

is humming, or

is pitching paper into the wastebasket.

Most salespeople continue talking. They're not getting anywhere. If your customer isn't listening, stop talking!

Point 5. Tips to help make you a better listener.

Listening is a fascinating and complex skill, and like

any other skill, it takes time to develop. I'll say a lot more about listening throughout this book, but right now, I'd like you to consider these points:

- Encourage your customer to talk by being a good listener. That's the only way you'll learn what the customer wants.
- Limit your talking. You cannot talk and listen at the same time.
- If you don't understand something, ask questions!

Too often we *don't* ask. How often do you go into a meeting where you don't have a clue to what's going on? You feel as if you walked into a baseball game at the 7th inning. Are you too embarrassed to say, "Excuse me, Sparky, what the hell are you talking about?" Most of us *don't* say that because we don't want to look stupid.

We act this way on a national scale. Think back to the Iran-Contra affair. Did *you* understand it? Do you know *any*one who *did?* Your customers don't want to look stupid, so they don't ask questions either. So you— and everyone else in your company—must ask your customers good questions to be sure your customers understand.

- Don't interrupt. Allow for pauses.
- Focus on what the customer is saying; shut out distractions. Try to get rid of them. If you're in a room that's really cold or hot, what are you thinking about?
- Take notes if possible to remember important thoughts. First of all, you can't remember everything a customer tells you. Second, it makes a really powerful impression on your customer.
- Occasionally, use interjections such as, "Yes... I see," to show the customer that you're listening and with him or her. Interjections encourage the

speaker to keep talking. The best interviewers on television do this; it says, "I'm listening," and it keeps the person talking.

- Don't jump to conclusions about what the customer will say. What's the first thing you think when *you* get back to the office and see a message to call a customer you just saw? You think, "They changed their mind! They're going to cancel the contract!" You finally get up the nerve to call, and what do they say? "You left your briefcase here." Just fax it to me.
- Verify information when necessary.
- Paraphrase what the customer has said to be sure the meaning you get is the meaning intended. Practice these examples (or similar phrases) until you can say them with zest, conviction, and enthusiasm for life:

    "What you're saying to me is...."
  or:
    "If I understand you correctly...."

Good listeners paraphrase. It works. You get the clarification you need, and the customer senses that you are listening. Paraphrasing is equally effective over the phone. Rephrase what you heard, then ask more pointed questions to determine the problem or what course of action to take.

- When necessary, ask questions for more information.
- Be willing to accept, without prejudice, the thoughts and opinions of your customer.
- Put the customer at ease. Help the customer feel free to talk.
- Develop the desire to listen. You have to want to listen before you hear and understand.

• Listen with a purpose to identify the important elements of what the customer is saying.

Point 6. Ask questions the way doctors do.

Approach your customer the way your doctor approaches you. It's your doctor's job to ask you questions, to find out what's wrong, and to fix it. You trust your doctor. Shouldn't it be the same thing in business? Absolutely!

Your doctor is a good listener. So is your dentist.

People tend to trust good listeners. When your dentist says you've got a cavity, do you doubt the fact? You say, "Go ahead, fix it." You want your customers to trust you in the same way.

Effective listening does not just happen automatically. You have to make it happen. To practice listening, you have to consciously tell yourself, "I'm going to listen." Most people are not good listeners. The people who are have *learned* how. Doctors and lawyers don't interrupt or think about what they're going to say next; they really focus on listening.

Point 7. Your job is to investigate and to satisfy the customer.

Your job is to make sure your customers are happy. Your focus is on the customer. Selling is an investigative process. It consists of finding out what the customer wants and, if you can, giving it to him or her. That's your job: dealing with people.

That's why most salespeople stink: they go out and sell without considering the customer's wants or needs. *That* is not selling. Real selling is an art form.

A progress check: what do you notice now about your style?

Take a moment to review what you have learned so far and what you have observed about your own personal listening habits:

- Did you catch yourself not listening as well as you should?
- Did you jump in with a comment before the speaker finished?
- Did you ask more questions?
- Did you make a list of questions before you went out on a sales call?
- If yes, did you pull out that list and actually *use* it during the call?

At first, you'll realize there are times you're not listening, or that you're making statements instead of asking questions. Just keep at it. As you work at it, you'll improve!

Some people have told me:

"I listened instead of worrying about what I was going to say next, which is what I usually do. And I got lots more information."

If you do that, you've saved yourself a lot of worrying! And instead of all the wear-and-tear of worrying, which is definitely *non*productive, you get some very productive results.

And some people have said:

"I started to jump in and interrupt, but then I waited a moment, and my prospect said what I was going to say."

It's much more effective when the buyer voices the conclusion!

And occasionally, someone even says:

"I started to interrupt, but I caught myself, and the customer gave me some totally unexpected information."

4

Confidence:
You Must Earn It. It's Worth It!

Point 1. The benefits of confidence

1. Confident people succeed.
2. People like to associate with confident individuals.
3. You feel better about yourself.
4. Others respect your knowledge or ability.
5. You grow—you move forward rather than falling back.

Confident people suceed.

If I walked in and said, "Uh, hi, I'll be your sales trainer. I think I'm giving you good information. Does it sound okay to you?" then people would say, "Hal, you're a memory, a vapor, Casper the Friendly Ghost. You're outta here."

Point 2. You have to earn it. And you can.

Confidence is something you must *earn*. You must pay your dues. It takes time and—usually—hard work to be efficient, fluent, or knowledgeable in whatever you desire.

The one and only way to master the art of confidence is to *explore*. Learn all you can about your subject. But above all, practice, practice, and then practice more.

We are all creatures of habit. When you face something new, you have to learn it, get comfortable with it. The only way to get confidence is to practice so you know your material cold. You have to want to be your best, to do the most.

If you are not comfortable in something, practice it, and you will become more comfortable in it!

Very few salespersons get their skills down pat. How well do you know *your* material? If you do, you'll impress your customer.

We respond to a person's confident attitude as much as we do to that person's actual skills. From what school did your dentist graduate? At the top of the class—or the bottom? Has anyone died in your dentist's chair? Are you sure your dentist can read your X-rays? Is your physician board certified? If you're like most people, you don't know. People stick with a doctor or dentist who is confident.

In my opinion the master of confidence is Lee Iacocca. He says, "I might be CEO of Chrysler, but basically I'm a salesman." What confidence! What salesmanship! He sold the Federal government on lending Chrysler millions of dollars. He sold the banks on lending millions more. He sold his employees on taking pay cuts.

Point 3. How to make a positive impression.

I still remember the first time I saw Bruce Springsteen perform back in the early 1970's. I sat transfixed for three and a half hours. I have never seen a more incredible show, and every show he put on was the same. Enthusiasm made him such an amazing talent. He loved to perform. He couldn't wait to play again.

Another example of enthusiasm is Michael Jordan. He made basketball fun. In fact he's just about the only basketball player who has a Love of Basketball clause in his contract so he can play in a pickup game any time, anywhere he wants. That love shows in his games.

Enthusiasm is an invaluable sales aid. I use it every day. When people come to my seminars, I'm selling them on me. I want them to say, "Wow! This Hal Becker is pretty good!"

How to do it.

- Use enthusiasm as a sales aid. Enthusiasm shows that you are confident about your product and proud of your company.
- Develop a winning attitude. You must believe that your company is the best, that it is the only one your prospect should buy from, and you must be prepared to back this belief with facts. To be a winner, you have to work for a winner. If you do not believe your company is the best, you shouldn't be selling it. If you get up every day and say, "I hate this company, and I hate what I'm doing," then I suggest you go to your boss and say, "Hal told me to tell you I quit." If you love what you're doing, *really* love it, then it's not work. Imagine how much fun you would have if you really like what you do every *day*. If you don't love what you're doing now, then I really suggest you quit it and do something you *do* love.
- Make the prospect feel important. Convince your prospects they will get all the attention they need

from you.

- Put your body into the sale. Shake hands firmly. Walk with assurance. Men and women both like a nice strong handshake. Develop an assured, take-charge posture with your voice and body. Be enthusiastic, and really get into what you're doing. We all like to be around persons who are up, not persons who are down.
- Use your voice effectively. Speak clearly and in a conversational tone. Smile. Speak economically; use only those words that state simply and effectively what you have to say. Try not to use big fancy words. All you do is lose people.

Confidence sells the buyer on you. And people buy from people.

Your prospect probably does not know your company or your product. The bottom line is whether *you* can sell the product. If your prospect doesn't know a lot about the company, the product, or the benefits, the issue will come down to one thing: price.

Point 4. Price is rarely the issue.

In business, price is *not* the overriding issue *unless* your customer is uninformed. True, we buy some things solely on price. That's why we have places like the Wholesale Club. We also have Saks Fifth Avenue because people want service. When you don't know much about what you're buying, you buy price.

But in business and other important issues, price rarely decides the issue. If you're sick and the surgery costs $1,500, you don't tell the surgeon, "Take $800 or I'll go somewhere else."

Even with products where we think price is the major factor, it really isn't. I demonstrate this in my seminars constantly. Hardly one person in 1,000 remembers to the dollar the price of a refrigerator or television set. And even with items where price is a factor, service is important.

If I sold you a VCR and I helped you set it up, where will you go when you need another appliance? You'll come back to me because I took good care of you. And if it costs $20 more at my store, you won't go elsewhere because you feel comfortable buying from me.

Pricing is usually pretty competitive. In business, you and your competitors are all pretty much in the same ballpark.

Think about your business. Basically, you do the same things as your competitors. What makes *you* different is *you.* And by you, I mean everyone, from receptionists to salespeople to technical support to people in the plant. Everyone has to work together to do what's best for the customer. That's how it has to be.

If you charge *less,* you better take something away. Otherwise you come across as foolish or dishonest.

You can charge *more* if you give more. That something more is usually something you *do,* service, something more than the customer expects. And the customer appreciates it.

Think about this situation: You've just finished an average meal, but the service was the best you've ever had. What do you do? You leave a generous tip. Is sales different? If you work harder for your customer than the competition does, then you should get more!

A look at where we discount—and where we don't.

You are in your favorite restaurant and have finished

the meal. The bill arrives: $26. You say to the waiter, "I'll give you $18 cash." Ridiculous? of course.

But when you walk into a car dealership, you expect to deal if you're buying a car. But when you walk 50 feet to the service department, you don't bargain over the mechanic's hourly rate of $44. Bargaining is not accepted in the service department.

That's not to say that one year or five or ten years from now, we might not find ourselves bargaining where we hadn't before, or vice versa. It's all a matter of what is socially acceptable, and society's idea of what's acceptable is changing constantly.

If you're buying something important to you but you don't know anything about the field, like computers, then you have two options—if you're smart. You can either bone up on the subject or else you can buy from an operation that can do it right for you. If you're uninformed and you walk into a wholesale type of place, you won't get the product or service you need.

Point 5. Testimonial: Confidence sells.
How else can the customer tell
how well the job is done?

One of the worst days in my life was the day my computer crashed. I had backed up the disks, but I thought I might screw the disks up. Do you know what that's like for a business owner? Deadly! My computer company came out right away to look at the hard drive.

They charged for that, and I gave them an extra $100, but I didn't mind because they took care of me right away. It was the greatest feeling. That's what the money's for, and that's what service is all about: going above and beyond the call of duty. You can think of plenty of examples like that.

Well, that company gave my name as a referral. What do you think I said when I was called for a reference?

I don't know if my programmer is good or not, because I don't know what a good programmer is or isn't, any more than I can tell you how my doctor or my dentist stacks up against other doctors or dentists. What I *do* know about my programmer and his company is that on one of the worst days of my life, when my system crashed, he was on my doorstep within an hour. I actually paid double what they billed—it was so important to me that their response time was so quick and that their attitude was so hassle-free and super. My entire company is based on a computer system, and if my computer shuts down, their good service literally saves the day for my company.

Stand tall!

You are no better and no worse than anyone else out there. If anyone tries to treat you like a doormat, don't let them! You don't have to let that happen.

Behave like an equal, and you'll be treated like an equal.

A lot of salespeople are uncomfortable around CEO's or celebrities. Let me explain something: their lives are no different than yours when they go home: they have the same problems, the same happiness, the same fears.

Do you have the eye of a tiger?

I've seen people who have the eye of the tiger. Whatever they go after, you know they're going to get it. They have assertiveness, aggressiveness. They're going to be unbelievable. In sales, as in anything in life, the key is finding the one thing you really love and doing it.

Point 6. Hal Becker's high-impact workout to build self confidence.

- Strengthen your character through self-reliance. Depend less on others. Your reward will be more self-confidence and more conviction in your actions.
- Resolve that your prospect will find you friendly.
- Learn to judge your prospect's mood.
- Form and strengthen good habits. Recognize undesirable habits and then weaken and break them.
- Look at your habits. Do they give you a good start on the selling day?
- Make it a habit to put your customer's welfare before your own.
- Develop habits of positive thought and action. Be optimistic. Optimism, like enthusiasm, is contagious. Expect your prospect to buy.
- Practice habits that refresh you spiritually and keep you mentally alert.
- Make a habit of courtesies.
- Develop the habit of preparing thoroughly before you call on customers. Ask yourself, "Have I acquired the habit of preparing myself thoroughly before calling on my customers?"

The final element in building self confidence is to have absolute trust in your company and your product.

If you do not feel your company is the best for the prospect's needs, you shouldn't be selling it.

It is extremely difficult to sell a product you do not believe in. You are a salesperson, not a con artist.

> *Do not confuse confidence with aggressiveness. Do not steamroller the prospect!*
> *Think positively! Remember that the key to self-confidence must come from within yourself.*

Point 7. How bad can it get?

I was driving down the street with a friend when I spotted a couch in the window of a furniture store. I went in, tried out the couch, bounced around on it. No salesperson approached. I got up, looked around, and in the back of the store, holding up the wall, was this guy in a *triple*-knit polyester suit. I'll call him Lou—short for louse.

Lou: "Yo! Can I help you?"

Hal: "How much is this couch?" (Remember, this is the lead item in the window.)

Lou: "I don't know." (And he's not moving a muscle to find out!)

Hal: "Can you find out?

Lou: (After some delay,) "It's $699."

Hal: "Does this fabric come in any other colors?"

Lou: "Here's the swatch book."

Hal: "This book's for International. I'm sitting on Broyhill."

Lou: "You want International. It has great coil action." (A feature, not a benefit.)

Hal: "What about Broyhill?

Lou "It's crap, junk. You don't want to buy it." (As a sales trainer I *live* for this. My adrenaline is pumping.

The blood vessel in my forehead is popping. My friend is thinking, "Oh, no..." and looking for something to crawl under.)

Hal: "Tell me, where do you go for lunch?"

Lou: (startled by this switch) "Huh?"

Hal: "When you want something fast, what do you get?"

Lou: "Uh, I go get a submarine sandwich down the street."

Hal: "How do you like it? hot or cold?"

Lou: (Confused,) "Hot."

Hal: "Do they heat it for you, or do you microwave it yourself?"

Lou: "I do it myself."

Hal: "Does the microwave have a dial, or does it have buttons?"

Lou: "Buttons."

Hal: "Which button do you press?"

Lou: "Three, for sandwiches and pot-pie."

Hal: "Well, obviously you should be working there in a striped apron, because you know more about making sandwiches than you do about selling furniture!"

5

The Use of Questions in Selling

Point 1. The art and absolute importance of using questions in selling.

This is the heavy pizza part of this book. This is everything. If you practice this, it will change the way you sell and the way you interact with people. It will change your life. This isn't new material. I've just simplified things which have been around forever. They are *so* important.

Above all else.

The number-one rule of human communication is: People prefer talking to listening. Look at your own experience. Who do *you* find more interesting to talk to; the person who talks intelligently about a number of different subjects while you listen, *or* the person who asks you a number of intelligent questions and listens to what you have to say?

There's no doubt about it, is there?

The ability to ask questions is an *absolute must* for successful selling. Without questions you can never find out what the prospective customer wants to buy, or even *if* he wants to buy anything. It is for want of good questions that poor salespersons find their presentations falling a mile wide of the mark. This applies to *every*one, to *you*, whatever your product or service.

Put yourself in the buyer's shoes and imagine that you need an attorney. You talk to two attorneys. The first, Jane, pulls out a legal pad, asks a lot of questions, and tells you her fee is $175. I come in, jot down a few notes on a cocktail napkin, and tell you my fee is $175. Which of us will you choose? It could be that Jane is a marshmallow in the courtroom and that I'm a barracuda, but you don't know that. You pick Jane because she impressed you as a person who is organized and on the ball.

Point 2. It's not cheating. It's being prepared

In school, we weren't supposed to go into tests with our notes. That was cheating. By the way, in a recent study of 6,000 graduate students at 31 schools, two thirds *admitted* cheating at least once.

But now you're in real life, and it is *not* cheating to have your notes—your questions, your reminders—in front of you. It *is* being smart: making sure you don't forget something important. Common sense tells you that if you don't write it down, you'll forget something important. If an attorney goes into a trial without a list of questions, she's likely to forget to ask a critical question which could lose the case.

If a doctor doesn't use his list of questions (heart, lungs, and so on), he could forget to ask about something vital to a patient. But salespeople go on calls without having all the questions written out. It's laziness. And they lose the sale.

Point 3. A fun aside: The art of conversation and your class reunion.

There are two places where it is constitutionally okay

to lie: in a singles bar and at your high school or college reunion.

Whether you were in the class of '52 or '92, you were either cool or you weren't. The guys who were cool are doing absolutely nothing now and talking about their past. The uncool ones—the guys with the plastic pocket protectors—are cool now because they decided to make it happen.

I had so much fun at my high school reunion! The first person who came up to me had been the most beautiful girl in high school:

She: "I'm modeling in New York City."

Me: "I'm living with my parents and on an allowance."

The second person:

She: "I live in Paris. I'm studying to be a mime."

Me: "I live in Paris, too!"

She: "Really? Where?"

Me: "A little street on the Left Bank, the Rue Jenesaisqua."

She: "What? I've never heard of it."

Me: "It's just a tiny street. I live above a bakery."

She: "What are you doing?"

Me: "I'm racing in the Budweiser 500. The time trials are tomorrow, and if you come to the pit, I'll have a couple of passes waiting for you."

She: "Cool! (Luckily for me, she didn't show up!)

The next person had been the smartest kid in our class, and president of everything—president of our senior class, president of Student Council, president of the Honor Society, president of the Nausea Club:

He: "I got my doctorate in microbiology, and I'm teaching at Northeastern U.

Me: "I got my doctorate in philosophy. Tell me, what

grants do you have? What's your favorite amoeba? Your least favorite? How do you spell paramecium? (All he had to do was ask me one question, like, "Who's Siddhartha?" and I would have been dead!)

That's a pretty extreme way of saying that questions make you appear interesting, but it's true.

Point 4. Questions give you the initiative. They give you control.

First, questions allow you to retain the initiative in the conversation. Obviously, if you're asking the questions, you hold the right to establish the subject under discussion. Similarly, the converstion will continue along the lines indicated by your questioning.

Second, questions give you control of the conversation. Just as you can influence the lines along which the conversation develops, so you can change the subject under discussion the moment you feel the conversation is heading in the wrong direction.

Then, if you want the person to stop talking altogether, all you need to do is ask a question that is answered yes or no. The prospect will not be upset even if you interrupt to ask this question.

Point 5. Questions allow you to tune in to your customer's style and needs.

Questions allow you to adapt your conversation and modes of expression to the characteristics of each person you talk to.

To sell well, you do not have to try to change your class or status or personality. You just have to ask the right questions, listen to the way the customer expresses himself or herself, and then reply using the same terms.

It is when you talk rather than listen and when you use terms that are unfamiliar to the customer that misunderstanding occurs and communication is lost.

Questions also clarify. Few people can express an idea fully in one or two sentences. You cannot take the risk of misunderstanding because you have incomplete information, so you must constantly check the customer's meaning by asking questions.

The questions that clarify meaning and establish understanding are the questions that begin:

Who...?   What...?   Where...?
When...?   How...?   Why...?

These are known as the five Ws (plus an H).

Point 6. You have the license to ask questions.

Why? Because whether you are making your call in person or by phone, you began your dialogue by saying, "May I ask you a few questions?"

With that preliminary, most people will answer as many questions as you care to ask and will not be upset by your questions. From repeated personal experience, I can assure you this is true.

And plenty of times people will tell you things they wouldn't or shouldn't normally tell you, such as what your competitor charges for a product.

Every person is different and every situation is different. Many people answer questions. Some people don't.

People who do answer questions will act differently depending on the situation. Here, as always, you have to pay attention for the signals. If it sounds as if the person is shifting in his chair, he may be getting a bit uneasy or impatient, and you should take your cue and let go.

Every one of your customers is different. You're different from every other salesperson. And every situation you walk into will be different. Watch for signals that tell you what's right for right now.

Point 7. The trial close: The question that establishes commitment.

You can use questions to establish the customer's commitment to a favorable decision. The technique you use is based on the conditional sentence:

"If I... then will you... ?"

For example:

"If I can give you a competitively priced program for the finest software and full service, would you be interested?"

Or:

"If I could find a way for you to pay your bill promptly, would you do it?"

You can see, therefore, that questions are essential to the sale. If you want to learn to sell and you don't know where to start, this is your first lesson:

Learn to ask questions. There is only one way to learn, and that is *by doing it.*

Try to go through the whole day making no statements but only asking questions. It will seem very awkward at first, but *persist!* With time and practice, it will get easier.

See for yourself how well you can make yourself understood by using questions in place of statements. There is not a statement that cannot be expressed as a question, even if all you can do is put the word "Surely" at the beginning of the sentence or the words "isn't it?"

at the end of the sentence.

If you have the determination to do this, you will quickly learn to restructure the way you communicate with people. And as you do it, you will notice the change in people's response to you. You will become a better persuader.

> *A top-flight salesperson can carry through an entire sale from beginning to end by making no statements and by only asking questions. You will really know how to ask questions if you can do the same!*

Point 8. How to use questions to probe for real wants and needs.

We are creatures of habit. The older we get, the more we resist change. Did your parents insist that they did not want cable television or a VCR? Did you force these things on your parents? What happened? Now your parents can't do without them!

How long ago did you get your first car with air conditioning? Before that, you insisted it was a luxury. Now would you ever consider a car without it?

Do you have a cellular phone? If you don't, I assure you that if I gave you one for just 24 hours, you'd be hooked.

Let's say that I sell compact-disk players for your car. I am talking to Joe:

Hal: "Do you have a compact-disk player at home?"

Joe: "Yeah! Love it."

Hal: "Do you really love digital sound?"

Joe: "I sure do. The sound in my home system is unbelievable, fantastic."

Hal: "Do you have a CD player in your car?"

Joe: "Oh, no. That's awfully expensive."

Hal: "If I could prove that the cost would be very little—pennies a day, and that you would notice much better sound over cassette tapes, would you be interested?" (This, by the way, is a trial close).

Joe: "I'd love that, but it sounds awfully expensive. How can it be pennies a day?"

Hal: "If you keep your car for two years, a CD player would cost about 50 cents a day. The total cost is $250, and spread over 24 months, with 22 business days in each month, that comes to 47 cents per day."

What do you think will happen? Notice that all the above is done only by asking questions. If Joe says he doesn't want the CD player, I would say:

Hal: "Could I stay in touch with you every couple months—no high pressure—just to find out about your wants and needs?" (that's salesmanship.)

It's like learning a foreign language.

If you have ever learned a foreign language, you know how hard you had to concentrate on it at first. Eventually, with practice, you could speak without thinking about it.

At first, thinking in questions will feel like a foreign language, but eventually you will be able to do it automatically. You only do well if you learn to think in questions. (See next page.)

Point 9. Taking the show on the road: The anatomy of a real live sales call.

Step #1: Operations.

When you go to a company, say, "Tell me about your

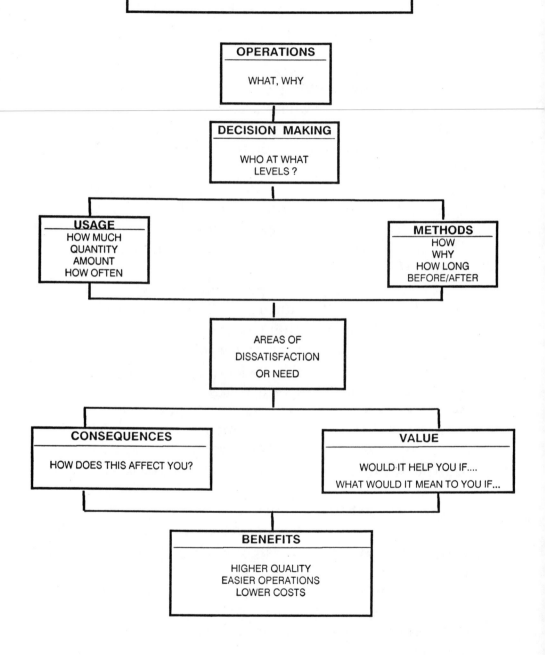

business." That question breaks the barrier between you
and the owner or representative. The owner will go on
and on. That business is a surrogate child, and the
owner is proud of it.

Step #2: Decision making

After you determine what the company makes, determine who is the decision-maker.

You have to make sure you're talking to the right
decision- maker. Always start at the top and work your
way down. Most salespeople don't want to deal with
someone high up in the organization. They take the
course of least resistance. They fear rejection.

But if you start too low, you may do yourself out of
the sale. Here's why:

Let's say that Greg is the president and Carol is in
charge of sales. I go first to Greg and ask, "Who makes
the decisions on sales training courses?" He says Carol
does, so I go to her and say, "Greg told me to talk to
you." Will she be receptive? You bet.

Let's say that instead I go first to Carol and she says
she's not interested. If I go over her head and talk to
Greg, he will tell me, "That's not my decision. See
Carol." Will she be resistant? Have I alienated her? You
bet! The way to make sales is to start at the top.

Yes, you can get to the top!

Most salespeople say, "You can't get through to the
CEO." This just is not so. The truth is: the higher up
you go, the nicer they are.

Always start at the top, unless the prospect calls you,
in which case let your contact person go through the
channels, even if it takes four times as long. It all comes
down to common sense.

"That decision is made by the board." Kiss of death—or opportunity?

How many times have you heard, "This decision has to go through a board." At this point, here's what a top salesperson does:

Hal: "Mr. Low, do you have an interest in this service we're selling? (Notice this is expressed as a question. Always think in question form.)"

Low: "Yes."

Hal: "I would like to offer this idea. When you present this product at your board meeting, all these people with big egos will probably ask a lot of questions. Some of those questions I could probably answer for you on the spot, right?"

Low: "Yeah."

Hal: "Would you like it if I came and sat in the hall, so if you need me, I'll be right there?"

Low: "That could work."

Hal: "If you put it on the agenda, I could be available to answer the board's questions directly. What do you recommend?"

Let me say this: I sit on two boards, and whether a company is profit or nonprofit, if the board really makes this decision, and if they know the company really needs something, they will want the salesperson to come in and field their questions directly.

If you don't ask, you will never find out whether you can get access to the board. I've heard people say, "If the board makes the decision, it's the kiss of death." Ask if you can go to the board meeting.

When you do go, and you're sitting in the hall, don't just sit. Take paperwork so the time is productive.

Notice that you are not going over your contact person's head. You are working with that person. Besides, it's your job to get access to the decision-maker.

Here's a bet you can win.

I wish I had $100 for every salesperson who tells me it's impossible to get to the CEO of large corporations. I've proven it can be done.

I once bet five dollars that I could get through to the CEO's of the three largest banks in Cleveland. I looked up the phone number of the executive office, asked for the name of the CEO, and called. The next thing I knew, the guy was on the other end of the line:

He: "What can I do for you?"

Me: "Nothing. I'm a sales trainer, and I bet five dollars that I could talk to you. I could send you a buck... it will double itself in 12 years."

There are two kinds of decision makers.

First, there is the real decision maker. And second, there's the queen for the day who says, "I'm in charge. I'm the fire-breathing dragon. nobody gets past me." If you get this person, ask her or him this:

"Who besides yourself also assists in the decision-making process?"

This lets the gate-keeper feel important and enables you to get the name of the person you need to talk to.

Step #3: Usage.

Once you've gotten in front of a decision-maker, you need to get some facts. What is the usage: quantity, stock, and so on?

Step #4: Methods.

What are the methods: How? Why? How long? What was it like before and after? Who do you use now? Why did you switch to this company?

Step #5: To get a prospect to switch to your product, look for dissatisfaction.

After you find out what product or service your prospect is using, your next step is to find areas of dissatisfaction or need.

If a prospect is completely satisfied and says, "We love our system," what should you tell them? "Thank you very much. I'll stay in touch. I'll give you a call every so often."

but more likely than not, you will find areas of dissatisfaction or need.

A magic question.

An excellent way to find an area of dissatisfaction is to ask:

If you could change anything about your present supplier, what would you change?

It's a magical question, and it works! Here's another example:

"Bob, if you could change anything about your present way of designing, what would it be? Is the size of screen important? Would it help if you could have a screen that's bigger or brighter, so the image is easier to see? Do you get eye fatigue? If you could go home at the end of the day with your eyes and head feeling bright and clear, would that be important to you?"

Step #6: Consequences.

For each area of dissatisfaction or need, look for consequences:

How does that affect you?

Step #7: Value.

Look for value:

What would it mean to you if...?

Would it help you if...?

To find these areas of dissatisfaction, you have to ask very specific questions:

Hal: "Mr. Customer, when you place a service call, how long is it before the company responds?"

Joe: "Eight hours. (This guy is used to poor service, and he doesn't even realize it! At this point the typical salesperson says: "Eight hours! that's terrible! We can do it in half the time." No!)

Hal: "Mr. Customer, when you get eight-hour response time, how does that affect you? (What are the consequences?)

Joe: "It means our system is down that long.

Hal: "What would it mean to you if I could cut that time in half? We'd guarantee you four-hour response time, and if you don't get it, WE will pay you. (What would the value of that be?)

Step 8: Benefits.

If the customer says yes to any of these, I can proceed to telling him or her about my product's benefits.

I suggest that you take a sheet of paper and write down all of your questions. I've enclosed a sample (see next page) for you. Make 50 copies, so you can use one with all your customers. Your customers will not be offended, I assure you.

Point 10. The flow chart and the girl of my dreams.

Let's apply this strategy to the world of dating:

Customer Profile   Date _____

Company _____   Phone _____

Division of _____   Contact/ Title _____

Address _____   Fax _____ After Hrs. # _____

_____   Referred by _____

Hrs/ Operation _____ Dock? _____   Decision Makers/ Title _____

Type of Business _____   _____

Operations
How long have you been with the company? _____ How many employees? _____

Other locations? _____

Decision Making
Who besides yourself participates in the decision making process? _____

_____

Usage
How much?

Quantity _____

Stock _____

Misc. _____

Methods
Current vendors/previous vendors?   How long?   Why?

_____   _____   _____

_____   _____   _____

_____   _____   _____

Dissatisfaction
What would you change about your current vendor if you could change anything? _____

_____

Consequences
How does this affect you? _____

_____

Value
What would it mean if I could provide? _____

_____

Benefits   • Higher quality   • Easier operations   • Lower cost

Notes _____
_____
_____
_____
_____
_____
_____
_____
_____
_____
_____
_____
_____
_____
_____
_____
_____
_____
_____
_____
_____
_____
_____
_____
_____
_____
_____
_____
_____
_____

Referrals - Persons in other departments who might benefit from our services

Name _____ Dept. _____ Phone _____

Name _____ Dept. _____ Phone _____

Name _____ Dept. _____ Phone _____

Results

____ Visit   Appointment date/ time _____

____ Send literature Date sent _____

Hal: "Would you like to go out for a cup of coffee?"

Sue: "No."

Hal: "Why not?"

Sue: "I've got a boyfriend."

Hal: "What's his name?"

Sue: "Jim."

Hal: "How long have you been dating him?" (Usage.)

Sue: "A year."

Hal: "What do you like most about Jim?"

Sue: "He's real cute."

Hal: "If you could change one thing about Jim, what would it be?" (Dissatisfaction.)

Sue: "He works too much."

Hal: "How does that affect you?" (Consequences.)

Sue: "He's just not available."

Hal: "What would it mean if you could meet a guy who's fun and cute and who's available all the time?" (Value.)

Sue: "Sounds good to me."

Hal: "Let me tell you about myself." (Benefits!)

You see what I did. I had a path, and my questions led her down that path.

An attorney in the courtroom knows exactly where he or she's headed the whole time. Attorneys have a lot of questions, and those questions are written out. Attorneys think in questions.

Programmers think in questions. Attorneys and programmers have made an art out of asking questions.

There are no right or wrong questions! The only thing that makes a true salesperson is the asking of questions.

When you, in selling, have practiced asking questions, it will be an art form for you too. Picasso Jones. Rembrandt Smith.

"You changed my life!"

A year or so ago, a guy came up to me and said, "Hal, I want to thank you for changing my life." I said, "Wait a minute, I didn't do anything. I just gave you the tools."

He said, "Hal, I've been a father for 16 years, and just in the past couple of weeks I've started sitting down with my kids and asking them questions instead of always *telling* them. I found out so much about my kids that it's changed the way I deal with them. *You* changed the way I deal with them."

Have I convinced you yet?

The only way with your boy friend or girl friend, husband or wife, kids or whomever is to ask questions. Communicate! Find out what they need. Your job in a relationship is to try to satisfy the needs of people around you and to make them happy and want to be around you. To have good friends, you have to be a good friend.

In business, the way to make your customers stay your customers is to continue to make them happy. To do that, ask them questions!

All questions are good. As you tackle each day and observe what happens, you will improve your questions.

Whatever discomfort you feel at first will disappear. It's like working out: your muscles get sore at first, and you doubt if you can do it. But eventually, it gets easier.

> *When you have mastered the art of asking questions, you will find yourself with the most powerful tool you could ever have.*

I cannot speak enough about this.

Point 11. Another proof: The art of cross examination.

You've probably never heard of Irving Younger, but he's the grandfather of cross-examination. He teaches trial attorneys how to be power attorneys. Six of the points he teaches to attorneys can be equally helpful to you:

1 Be brief.
2. Use short questions in plain words.
3. Always ask a leading question.
4. Listen to the answer.
5. Don't quarrel with the witness.
6. Save the ultimate point for your final argument.

Does this sound at all familiar?

Consider this: law school does not teach people to become attorneys. It teaches them to think analytically and how to do research. They learn to become attorneys by going into practice—and *practicing*. We learn how to become salespeople the same way—by practicing.

Point 12. Simplify!

In my seminar I include a page of the most complicated flow charts and obscure language possible. And I tell my people, "This is garbage. It can be reduced to the simplest everyday terms, which is what I did in the flowchart on page 57."

You can do things in one of two ways. You can make things easy or you can make them hard. Strategic planning. Organizational needs. Technical gobbledygook.

How do *you* want to do things? My vote is that you go through life making things easy—for yourself, for your customers.

To make things easy, ask questions. If you are in customer support, ask questions, diagnose the problem,
and correct it. If you are in sales, ask questions to find
out what the customer needs and how you can help.

Point 13. Make Columbo your hero.

If people were to pick a movie star who looked the
part of the supersalesperson, most people would pick
someone smooth and debonair, like James Bond. David
Sandler, the sales trainer extraordinaire, says the supersalesperson would look like Columbo, the detective.
Columbo appears rumpled, absent-minded, and awkward. Suspects think Columbo is stupid and bumbling
until he reveals their guilt.

Columbo makes no assumptions. He doesn't try to
read other peoples' minds. He gets what he wants by
asking questions. Then he asks more questions, and
more questions. And when he says, "Let me ask you just
one more question." that's usually when he solves the
case.

If you have only one list, this is it.

We all make lists. Some people get so carried away
they make lists of lists. Well, here's one list you
absolutely need: the questions you will ask your next
customer or prospect.

Why is this list so important? Because listening is
important. And you can listen a lot more if you ask
questions, *good* ones. To do this, you've got to *have*
questions—not just some vague fuzzballs drifting
around in your gray matter, but specific questions. To
nail them down, you have to make a list.

Notice I didn't say your list has to be *complete* or *perfect*. You will think of more questions when you walk into a prospect's office. And over the days, weeks, and months ahead, you'll think of new questions, better questions, unpredictable questions.

When you walk into a company, a store, a prospect's office, keep your eyes and ears peeled for new questions that can help you in this specific situation.

Then, when you're face to face with your customer or prospect, pull out that list. Use it!

When I start working with a new group, people are reluctant to do this. Maybe it goes back to our seventh-grade history class—if we prepared and brought in notes, we were cheating. Well, we're now in the real world, and a list of questions is *not* cheating. In fact, it has the opposite effect. Your customer thinks, "Wow, this guy Hal takes his work seriously. He's put thought and effort into it. He wants to know what I think."

So, while I work at listening, I also predispose the customer or prospect to pay attention to me and my product. *You* can do the same thing.

Asking questions: The only way to sell.

There is only one way to sell. Period. That is to ask questions, to probe, and to qualify your prospects. I don't care what course you take or who teaches you, that is the only way to sell. On that foundation you build your style, your personality. You start with questions.

You're not going to change overnight. Today you'll do a little more and a little better than you did yesterday, and you'll try one thing different from what you've done before. Tomorrow you'll improve a little bit on what you did today, and you'll try one more new thing.

That's how you achieve your goal of being one of the best. You don't have to be super-smart or super-talented. You don't have to have the most unique and wonderful product ever developed in the history of the universe.

The only thing you have to do is to work at asking questions and listening.

The only way to sell, period, is to ask questions and to qualify your prospect. There is no other way. none. It is the only way to sell.

In the first session of my seminar, I make a big point about asking questions. At the second session, I invariably find that almost nobody has started doing this yet. No matter what company I go into, this happens. And it happens to every sales trainer.

Everything else about selling is based on your style, your personality, and how you create your own art of salesmanship.

So start asking questions. Then ask more questions and better questions. The only way to better yourself is to do a little bit more than you have been doing and to try something different. Otherwise you'll continue along the line of what you do now, which is average or below average.

> *I cannot say it often enough! The only way to sell and the only way to keep your customers happy is by asking questions. Everything else is personality or style. I cannot be like you, and you cannot be like me. But you can be as successful a salesperson as I have been.*

Point 14. Remember Dale Carnegie?

As I've said, the techniques of sales have been well-known for a long time. In 1936 Dale Carnegie set down a number of ways to win friends and influence people. His ideas have been around a long time, but they still apply today. Six of his ideas are appropriate to sales:

- The only way to get the best of an argument is to avoid it. If you argue with a customer, you'll lose.
- Show respect for the other person's opinion; never tell him he's wrong.

To this I add: Never knock the competition or another salesperson. Here's how not to do it:

Seller: "What type of insurance do you have?"
Buyer: "Term.
Seller: "Term?! How long have you had that junk?"
Buyer: "Fifteen years."
Seller: "Fifteen years? I don't believe it!"
Let's replay that:
Seller: "What type of insurance do you have?"
Buyer: "Term."
Seller: "I see. How long have you had it."
Buyer: "Fifteen years."
Seller: "That was a great decision back then. Let me tell you about whole-life insurance."

You see the difference. The second salesperson is an artist who paints a very different picture from a totally different perspective.

- If you are wrong, admit it quickly and emphatically. Most people cannot do this. A real professional can.
- Let the other person do a great deal of the talking.
- Try honestly to see things from the other person's viewpoint.
- Be sympathetic to the other person's needs and desires.

6

Overcoming Objections

Point 1. How to understand and handle objections.

An objection is a form of disapproval. Do not view objections with fear; do view them as opportunities. That's so important I want to repeat it:

An objection is an opportunity.

By voicing objections, your customer tells you his or her needs and concerns.

Point 2. Techniques that help you deal with objections.

- Be relaxed while dealing with an objection. The customer is not confiscating your first-born child. There just happens to be a problem somewhere. Find out what it is. Being relaxed allows you to focus on the real issue and to deal with it more effectively.
- Determine the real objections by listening carefully. Clarify that you understand the objection by paraphrasing it. Probe the objection by asking key questions.
- Allow the customer to talk without interrupting. Sometimes people talk themselves out of an objec-

tion. This can happen even when a customer is so upset that he is ranting and raving. Let him talk, and he'll very likely talk himself out of that very objection. It does happen. All people want is to be taken care of. That's it.

- If the objection is vague, translate it into understandable issues.
- Never allow an objection to develop into an argument.
- Convince the customer that you understand how he or she feels.
- Never ignore a customer's objection.
- It is not necessary to agree with a customer's objection. Unresolved objections can be time bombs. If you and your spouse have an argument, would you go to bed mad? If you do, the problem is still there the next morning, but bigger. You go to work, write and rewrite what you're going to say. But when you get home, guess what: the house is gone. She took it. If a customer has a problem, take care of it now. Convince him that you understand how he feels. Restate the objection in your own words so there's no misunderstanding. You can't afford one.
- Be prepared for objections so you are not caught off guard.
- Have the ability to acknowledge and to counter objections.
- Develop a positive attitude regarding objections rather than displaying fear or irritability.
- Be attentive, not defensive.
- The best way to handle an objection is to listen politely and to show empathy. Problems do not go away by themselves.

Point 3. Gang up on objections.

Here's an effective way you can deal with objections. It's also more fun—remember, I did say we were going to have more fun!

Get your staff together: sales, other managers, support staff, technical. The more, the better. Start the ball rolling with a common objection, such as, "It's too expensive." Have everyone write down, in just a couple lines, how he or she handles that objection. Then pass the comment to the next person, who reads it to the group.

You'll find yourself saying, "Wow, I like the way she said that." The content may be similar to yours, but you may like the way it's packaged. You'll find, by the way, that you get the freshest ideas from new people.

Point 4. Why do you want objections? Consider these amazing facts

Of all sales, 63% are made after the *fifth* rejection. You need to hear five nos before you hear a yes.

But 75% of all salespeople give up after their first rejection.

That explains why 25% of the sales force often produces 95% of the results.

Every day, thousands of sales are made to customers who previously said no.

The only road to success in selling is to overcome objections and to sell on the basis of benefits to the customer.

Point 5. When the girl of my dreams says no.

1. Charlene keeps saying no when I ask her to go out.
2. Charlene has a boy friend.

3. Every six months I call Charlene. She's the girl of my dreams.
4. In the next six months she and her boy friend may split. I want to be ready if and when they do!

When the customer says no.

Stay in touch with your prospects. People don't mind it when a great salesperson does this:

Ms. Customer, would it be okay if I keep in touch with you, if I call you back in six months or so?

A last thought on the subject.

Every day thousands of sales are made to people who said no when first asked to buy. An objection is merely a roadblock which must be cleared away. If you are prepared, you will be able to answer these objections without hesitation or embarrassment.

Therefore, do not object to objections. They are a good sign that the customer is listening and thinking about what you are saying.

When your customer objects, that is only a human reaction: we first think about why we should not be interested; only then do we start to consider why we should be interested.

7

Cold Call Selling

Point 1. There are only two ways to get new business, and they aren't marketing and advertising.

To get real, live clients, you have to do one of two things: either knock on doors or use the telephone to get an appointment.

The best insurance.

Of all the various misfortunes that can befall a salesperson, one of the worst is to run dry of prospects. The best insurance by far against this calamity is cold-call selling. It's the only way to acquire and meet new business prospects. All that is necessary is to go out and call on total strangers.

The salesperson who consistently makes cold calls will excel. He or she has absolutely no influence, no pull, no mutual acquaintance that can be of assistance with a cold prospect. Cold-call selling is an excellent way to experiment and to develop and strengthen your skills. At the same time, it's a very profitable method of acquiring and developing new customers.

Point 2. Cold-call approach: When you really want to dance.

Think back to the dating scene. I go into a bar, and a band is playing a song I love. So I go up to this gal and ask, "Do you want to dance?" She says no. What should I do if I really want to dance this song? I have to ask someone else. She says no. I keep on going. Eventually someone will say yes. If I keep asking, I have a much better chance of finding someone who says yes.

Show me something different in sales. Isn't it the same thing?

You always hear that you've got to have prospects. Well, that means you have to go out and make calls on people.

Consider it a game.

Selling is a game. By that I mean that you shouldn't take it so seriously that you take rejection personally. If you take rejection of any sort personally, you'd better re-evaluate your view, because unless you've done something wrong, the person is not criticizing you personally—the person just doesn't want to deal with the situation.

Some salespersons are frightened by the thought of cold calling. Their reasons include an embarrassment over hearing *no,* which they equate with failure, and a history of past attempts which produced little success. Both these reasons are misconceptions.

Point 3. The truth about Babe Ruth.

I just learned this fact about the Home Run King. I wish I'd known this years ago, but then we're all learning constantly.

Babe Ruth was the Home Run King: 714 home runs. But what you don't hear is the number of times he struck out. What do you think *that* number is? 714? 1,014?

In the course of his career, Babe Ruth struck out 1,330 times. That's almost twice as many times as he hit home runs! You don't hear about his strikeouts, do you? You hear about his home runs. But he couldn't set that record for home runs without swinging at a lot of pitches and without striking out.

So, if you need to get a lot of sales, you need a lot of prospects. But to get a lot more prospects, you have to hear no a lot more often. When I was at Xerox, I learned to tell myself: Hal, if you want one more sale, one more *yes,* you need two more strong prospects. To get those two prospects, you need to hear *eigh*t people say *no.*

I made a *game* out of it. One of the things that really helped me personally was that I didn't take it *too* seriously. I didn't take rejection personally.

Ask yourself this very important question: do *you* take rejection, any sort of rejection, personally? If you do, I strongly suggest you re-evaluate the situation. Either you have to stop taking rejection personally, or you need to get into a different field.

Remember: rejection is as vital a part of sales as breathing. Knowing that, you're ready to get started on cold calling.

Point 4. Which is better: In person or by phone?

As I said, you have two ways to make cold calls: in person or on the phone. In my opinion, both ways are

equally good. Each way has its advantages and limita-
tions, so a lot depends on your own style and what
works well for you, your territory, and your product or
service.

Calling in person can be more fun because you can
see people and interact with them directly. Also, it's
harder for a prospect to tell you no face-to-face. On the
phone it's easier for the prospect to say no, but you can
make a lot more calls in a shorter period of time.

Whatever you choose, in person or by phone, choose
what you truly *enjoy*. When you enjoy something,
you're better at it.

Maybe you enjoy using the phone and you've never
tried knocking on doors. *Try* knocking on doors. If you
give it your best try and still don't like it, go back to
using the phone.

Above all, remember this about cold calls: you're
going to hear a lot of people say no. You might have to
knock on 20 doors to get two prospects, and only *one*
will buy. But that's what it takes.

Point 5. How many cold calls do you make each day? Consistency counts!

If you were in outside sales and if I were your manager, I would want you in the field from 9 a.m. to 4 p.m.
every day, because then—unless your territory is Utah—
you could make 15 calls every day. Most people in outside sales *don't* do that—they do a lot of other things to
put off making those calls. They like to sell, but they
don't like to make sales calls.

My success at Xerox was plain and simple. What
made me #1 in a field of 11,000 when I was 22 years
old? Are you ready? I didn't work smarter (because

I wasn't smarter). I just worked *harder*. I made 20 cold calls a day, 100 a week. *No* exceptions.

Again, consistency counts. If I want a great body, I won't get anywhere if I go to the gym for three hours today and then I don't go back for another three or four months. I have to go to the gym three times a week and work out just 45 minutes each time, and in three or four months I'll definitely see a change.

If you schedule a lot of calls today in one all-out effort and then not do anything for the next three months, you can't expect to become an unbelievable superstar.

But if, every day, you just do a little more and a little different, then in three months you're going to have a very nice prospect base.

The key to selling, like anything else, is consistency. If I were your manager, I would expect 10 new prospecting calls a day. Whatever you are selling, that is a realistic number. If you make only 8 calls today, then you have to make 12 tomorrow. It's not tough. But it's consistent.

It translates into 50 calls a week, 220 calls a month, and about 2,500 calls a year. That's a pretty good number.

Out of those 220 calls, *only* 5% are prospects. That's ten new prospects a month. People usually close between 40 and 50% of their prospects. Imagine what would happen to your company's business and your income if you add five new customers every month!

Point 6. Smarter, okay. Harder, yes!

I'll tell you a secret. I'm not that great a salesperson. I didn't have the right look. I didn't dress the best.

I wasn't the quickest or the smoothest of all. Far from it. So how could I become number one? I did just one really simple thing:

I worked harder.

We always hear, "Work smarter." Well, that's common sense. But most people don't want to work hard. That's what separates the winners from the losers.

When I talk about working harder, I don't mean you should kill yourself. All I mean is doing a little bit every day. Those numbers add up, believe me.

Absolute, total conviction.

The key to successful cold call selling is a positive attitude and absolute conviction. If you know nothing about the person you are calling on except his or her name, you have no idea whether he or she needs your product or service.

You must perceive the prospect as a person with a problem you can help solve *or else* your attitude will defeat your efforts from the start. You must totally believe in what you are trying to sell. The prospect wants to see this enthusiasm generated; it stimulates his or her interest and thinking.

That means you don't passively take *no* for an answer. When you hear *no,* you probe. You ask *why?*

Timing.

Good timing is an important factor in the success of any call. Keep in mind your prospect's work habits. Call at a time when you are less likely to be made to wait.

Is 8:30 a.m. Monday morning a good time to call? Of course not.

The actual making of a cold call presents two problems that need to be solved: getting to the right person, and receiving that person's attention and interest.

Even though there's no rule for getting in to see Mr. or Ms. Right, some basic methods and suggestions can help.

Point 7. The screen: About secretaries, receptionists and switchboard operators.

Usually, the persons who can help you the most are the secretary, receptionist, and switchboard operator. They can help you determine whether your prospect is the right person to see.

But first you must make a good first impression and try to win their cooperation. The greeting should not be familiar, patronizing, or arrogant. Use sincere, direct expression and a friendly smile.

How do you greet her? You want to be
> friendly,
> direct, and
> sincere.

You do *not* want to be
> familiar,
> patronizing or
> arrogant.
> Treat her as
> an equal and
> a normal person.

If you regularly have trouble with the gate keeper, then I suggest you check your attitude against the checklist above.

A lot of people talk down to the receptionist. They consider her unimportant and think that her job is to keep them out. These same salespeople hate to be treated like dirt. So why do salespeople treat receptionists so poorly?

It's no wonder that most receptionists are so tired of salespeople! It's up to you to show the receptionist she should let you in rather than keep you out.

A woman in one of my seminars said:

"I see this in my own work. I sublease space, and the way the office is set up, a lot of people think I'm a receptionist because of where my space is located. Those people treat me one way at first, and when they find out I have my own company, they treat me altogether differently."

Point 8. Screens were not born yesterday.

When you make a cold call and the screen asks you, "What is the purpose of your call?" what do you say?

"It's personal."

"Just say Joe Blow is here."

"It's confidential."

"I'm with the IRS."

"I'm with the Secret Service."

Some salespeople believe that disclosing their business to a screen will lessen their chance of getting to see the decision- maker. They resort to evasions. These tricks, however, do not fool the screen, who has seen and heard them many times. The screen is there to do a job. Cooperate with her, and she will most likely cooperate with you.

Remember:
- If you cooperate with the screen, she will cooperate with you. It's the Golden Rule, folks.
- All of us are just humanoids trying to do our jobs. The screen is a human being, just like you and me.
- All of us want to be around people who do their

jobs as best they can. You feel this way, and so does the screen.

Tell the screen *who* you are, *what* company you represent, and *how* your product or service can benefit her company.

The screen knows which executive is responsible for every function in the company, and she can steer you in the right direction. Consider her as a friend and ally on future calls.

Approach the screen with the realization that part of her job is to eliminate those callers who do not deserve their boss's valuable time. It's best to make the screen feel it's important to get you *in* rather than to keep you *out*. It boils down to convincing the screen that your product and service can benefit the boss.

What's the worst thing that can happen? The screen doesn't want to let you in. You can't get on her good side. She puts up a brick wall, and she's *not* going to let you in.

What if there's no way to get past the screen? The best way is to call when she's not there. Find out what time she goes to lunch, and call then. Or call at the times when you're likely to find only the decision maker in: after 5 p.m.

Point 9. Work while you wait.

What do you *do* when you're waiting in the reception area? Most salespeople watch television, if there is one, or leaf through popular magazines.

What *should* you be doing? Prepare for the call! There are many ways to do this:

- If there's something in the lobby about the company, read it!

- Review your questions.
- Look around you and see if there's something you can ask about or work into your presentation. For example, companies that belong to the Chamber of Commerce usually hang a plaque in the lobby. I know that members of Cleveland's Chamber of Commerce get a 20% discount on air time from a cellular phone company. If I worked for that company and I saw a Chamber of Commerce plaque in the lobby, I would use this fact in my presentation. Notice I do this in question form: How long have you been a member of the chamber of commerce? Are you a member in good standing? Are you aware of the great discounts and other benefits you can receive by being a member?
- And remember the receptionist is a great source of information. If you develop rapport with her, she can help you tremendously.

Point 10. Your cold call is not a sales call.

Above all, remember that the purpose of a cold call is *not* to sell the prospect on the spot. Your purpose is to gather information.

If the person you want to see is out, don't try to sell to someone else in the hope that person will convey your message and make your sale for you. A lot of salespeople think this is okay, but it doesn't work! Nobody can represent your company and your product to your prospect the way *you* can.

But if the prospect is out, you *can* get some good information from another person and use it the next time you call your prospect.

Make the most of precious time.

Tell me: How much time do people in outside sales actually spend in front of decision-maker prospects on a typical day?

30 minutes?

45 minutes?

One hour?

An hour and a half?

If you are in outside sales and are working in the field all day, then in a typical eight-hour day, you spend only one and one-half hours in front of decision makers. That's all!

Not much time, is it? That means you have two choices: One: You can prepare yourself and have better questions. Two: You can wing it and know that you're going to get stuck.

Point 11. You can learn a lot on 1,400 tours.

I figure that I've made 14,000 cold calls (never mind the arithmetic that got me there). I also figure that I've toured at least 10% of those companies, or some 1,400 tours.

If you do that, something terrific happens. First, you learn a little about a lot of subjects and businesses. You can use some fact out of all that when you start a conversation with a customer. And customers are impressed when you know something about their business.

Get a tour of as many places as you can. Your prospect will love it. The business is his baby, and he wants to show it to you. The key is that you have a sincere interest, and I emphasize the word *sincere*.

You can't walk through a place and not learn something. And learning is what cold calling is all about: you're knocking on doors, asking for a few minutes so you can ask some questions and make an appointment for later.

Point 12. When to take a rain check.

Getting in front of the decision-maker is such an achievement that most salespeople will charge ahead rather than recognize when they would be better off if they took a rain check.

You're in front of the decision-maker, who:

Starts to make a grocery list,

starts signing things,

goes through the mail,

looks at a magazine,

picks lint off her suit, or

is preoccupied by an emergency.

Most salespersons just proceed with their pitch, thinking "This will only take a couple minutes." They've come to sell, and nothing's going to stop them—except themselves.

If the decision-maker is preoccupied by other tasks or is battling alligators in the swamp, that decision-maker certainly isn't listening to you and certainly isn't about to buy anything. What can you do?

Hal: "Ann, I see you're pretty busy this morning. Why don't we reschedule, if that's okay with you!"

Ann: "Great! Is next Monday good for you?"

Hal: "Fine..."

When I see her next Monday, she'll have a lot more respect for me, and my relationship with her will start off on the right foot.

Point 13. How would you like to get six days work done in five?

You can get an extra day's worth of time—one and

one-half hours—in front of decision-makers each week *by spending* just 15 more minutes every day in front of decision-makers!

Point 14. Bob's Secret.

When I was at Xerox, one of the top salespeople was Bob Merkle, a guy who got a doctorate in psychology and then decided he'd rather sell than teach.

Bob's territory—this was back in the late 1970's—was an area that had only two big businesses, and all the other businesses revolved around those two. His territory was especially hard-hit by the recession, and one of the two big businesses closed.

You couldn't find a less promising territory, but Bob was always one of the top five salespeople.

The only time Bob brought in orders was Monday morning. He always set his closing appointments for Friday afternoon. Why do you think he did that? Bob had a clear field. All his competition had quit working for the week.

Think of the times when you can't seem to find anyone to take your money.

Think about what *you* do if *you* want something late in the day at the end of the week. You go to three stores, and two of them are closed. You're ready to buy, but you can't find anyone who'll take your money. When you want something, you want to make a decision and get on with your life.

Unless whatever you're buying is pretty basic on the hierarchy of needs, you don't actually *need* it. You *want* it. You might need transportation; you want a car. You might need clothing; you buy what you want to wear.

You might need a computer; you want a system. Always remember: we are selling wants, not needs.

Point 15. My favorite blizzard.

In 1978, when I worked for Xerox, we had the worst blizzard in Cleveland in 25 years. For three days visibility was zero. All the businesses were closed, including Xerox.

I had the best sales of my life during that blizzard.

At first I sat in my apartment and watched television. I got bored real fast. I was 22 years old, and I said to myself, "This stinks." I put on a flannel shirt and jeans, bundled up in a jacket and boots, and went out to knock on some doors.

Who do you think I found in the offices? All the receptionists and secretaries were at home. When I knocked on the door, I heard the boss say, "Come on in." All I could think was, "Wow! Really?" Every other time I'd only gotten as far as the lobby.

I walked in, and the first thing the boss said was, "Would you like some coffee?" I thought, *"Wow! All this and coffee, too?"*

Those three days I sold 23 machines—a record that still hasn't been topped.

The only reason I sold so many machines was that I was able to see so many decision-makers, and all I had to do was ask them some questions.

Think a moment about those decision-makers sitting in those offices during those three days. Guess what they were doing. Nothing! The secretaries weren't there to type letters or retrieve things from the file. There was no point in getting on the phone because hardly anyone was working.

Now if these decision-makers have a problem on a normal day, can they have confidence in me? Absolutely!

Point 16. How to use the telephone in cold calling.

Keep in mind that you are using the phone to get an appointment. The following tips are based on that fact.

Don't reveal too much.

Remember your objective: you use the phone to get an appointment. That's *all*. You are not going to close any deal on the phone. The longer you spend on the phone, the less your chance to make an appointment and ultimately to make a sale. If I want a date with Sue, I do *not* say this on the phone:

Hal: "Hi, Sue, my name is Hal. Bill gave me your name and I wanted to see if you'd like to meet me for a cup of coffee. I'm 5 foot 1, I weigh 182 pounds, and I drive an orange Yugo." (What's Sue going to say? "Sorry, I'm playing Parcheesi with my grandmother.")

I *do* say:

Hal: "Hi, Sue, my name's Hal. Bill gave me your number and maybe you'd like to go out and get some coffee for maybe half an hour. What's a good night for you?"

She's more likely to say yes. Show me what's different in selling.

Take advantage of the personal qualities of the phone call.

Refer to the prospect by name whenever possible. Focus on known needs or dissatisfaction.

Think about the American Express commercials for their credit card. They project warmth. They say, "We're here to take care of you. Our operators are standing by." It's all warm and fuzzy. I find this commercial totally unrealistic, not just of American Express, but of the general attitude toward customer service in America.

In real life, the phone rings 80 times or you get a string of automated messages before a human being comes on the line. You say something like, "I lost my card," and you hear, "Hold, please." Then you're hanging again in instant and total limbo.

But we want to be taken care of. When someone calls your company, your receptionist makes a first impression for the entire company. To the caller, she *is* the company. If she's rude, abrupt, or in a bad mood, the caller thinks your company is bad.

Don't conduct a one-sided conversation.

Give the prospect an opportunity to respond. Use open-ended questions or else force responses with either-or type choices.

Don't block objections.

Limit your goal to getting the appointment, not to solving your prospect's problems over the phone. Use objections as another reason to get together.

Don't accept a stall.

If a prospect wants to put off the decision, go back to the beginning and suggest another time. If a prospect had no need for your product, he would have already told you so. You seldom lose a sale by pushing a wishy-washy prospect.

Smile!

That's most important when you're on the phone, just as it is when you're face to face. A smile is a ray of sunshine. Feel that ray going through the fiberoptics of the telephone! Put a mirror in front of you to see if you are smiling. People love to be on the phone with some-one who's warm and friendly.

**If you're talking to the screen, ask,
"What's your name?"**

That way, when you call, you can say, "Hi, Beth. This is Hal." And *talk to* her; treat her like a human being.

When you're on the phone, never hang up first.
You know how it feels when someone hangs up on *you*.

Avoid starting with small talk.

I don't like it when someone, particularly a stranger, opens with "How ya doin'?" It's small talk. It's not the point of the call. If we want to schmooze or have a lit-tle bonding, we can do it later. You're calling me for a reason, so let's get down to business. Also, if you're going to engage in small talk, make it sincere.

Realize that you can't change wishy-washy prospects.

You know this type: he won't say no but he won't say yes. You cannot push someone who is wishy-washy into deciding for or against your product. A person who is wishy-washy will always be that way. A person who can't make a decision just is not going to do it. You can't force people to do things they don't want to do. It's equally pointless to worry about them.

Case history: Successful phone technique.

If I called you and said, "Hi, I'm Hal with ABC Life Insurance Company." what would your response be? You'd say, "I'm not interested." That's the *wrong* approach. Here's the right one:

Hal: "Hi, I'm Hal with ABC Life Insurance Company. I'm not selling anything now, I'd just like to ask you three quick questions. I'll only take 30 seconds."

You: "Well, okay."

Hal: "Do you have life insurance?"

You: "Yes."

Hal: "Can I ask what type you have—whole, term, universal?

You: "I have term."

Hal: "How much are your payments?"

You: "$500 a year."

Hal: "If we could meet and if I could show you that you could have additional benefits at a competitive price, would you be interested?"

Point 17. A great phone technique with the screen.

A difference in script can make a big difference in results. Here's what usually happens to most salespersons:

Hal: "Good morning, this is Hal. Is Ben in, please?"

Ann: "What company do you represent?"

Hal: "I'm with Direct Opinions. Is Ben in, please?"

Ann: "Will you tell me what this is about."

Hal: "It concerns some previous correspondence. I'd like to discuss it with Ben."

Ann is screening me out, isn't she? Try this instead:

Hal: "Good morning, is Ben in, please? Thank you!"

In most cases, when you say, "thank you", it's like a putting a period the size of a Buick at the end of your sentence.

Try this technique. You'll be pleasantly surprised at how well it works without being rude. "Is Ben in, please? Thank you." People don't expect it and they don't automatically use their usual responses.

It's a fun thing to try. Again, selling is a game of wits and of constant experimenting to see what will work.

Do you play a board game—chess, checkers, backgammon? If so, your object is to outmove the other person, fairly and squarely. There's a parallel in sales. You're trying to take the prospect in a certain direction while finding out what their needs are. Isn't that a doctor's or an attorney's job?

Point 18. Fax Becker.

Recently I wanted to put a fax line in to my house, where I already have business lines and personal lines. So I called Ohio Bell. The phone rang and rang, and then I sat on hold. Finally, when I got to talk to a human being about what I wanted, I was told, "I'm sorry, you have too many lines." Click. Dial tone.

I was more than a little upset. I called back and said, "Supervisor, please." At this point I had invested ten minutes in this call, and I was a little edgy.

The supervisor heard me out, then said, "I'm sorry. You have so many lines. What is this one for?"

I don't know about you, but I figure it's nobody's business what this line is for. Now I was mad, and there was no way I would tell her. I said, "My niece is moving in, and she needs her own phone line." The supervisor said, "Okay."

She took the order, and then asked, "How do you want your niece listed in the phone book?" I hadn't thought about that! "Her name is Faxine, but all her friends call her Fax." And so if you look in the Cleveland phone book, you'll see a listing for Fax Becker.

P.S. Six months later, a piece of junk mail with Ed McMahon's picture on it came to my house addressed to Fax Becker. Do you think a fax machine can win $10 million in a sweepstakes?

Point 19. A strategy for under a buck for prospects who won't return your calls.

You call the manager who says, "Oh, yeah, get back to me next week." You wait a week. You call again. The manager says, "I'm still interested. Get back to me in a week." Or else you just can't ever reach this person again. Here's what I did.

My first strategy was to fax this to the prospect:

Please check one box telling why you cannot call me back:

❑ I'm too busy but I'm still interested.

❑ I think you're a jerk, and I wish you'd just go away.

❑ Not returning your call is a power play, but if you beg me enough, I'll call you back.

❑ I never got your messages.

❑ I lost your messages.

❑ Other: _____

If you send this to people, what do you think they'll do? They'll laugh, and then they'll call you or send the fax back. Or maybe they'll take your call.

When I did this, it was creative, different. Also, I counted on the fact that most people have a sense of humor.

Point 20. Another technique that works and costs less than a buck.

Back in 1980 my third car was stolen. All my three cars had been American. I was so fed up with having my cars stolen that I decided, "I'll buy an import. Nobody will steal *that.*"

Shortly afterward, the dealership called to ask if I was satisfied. I was *so* impressed, and I told them,

"Thank you. We're all too quick to complain." I asked a few questions and learned that the dealership had homemakers making calls for them.

Neon lights went on in my head: what a great idea for a business on a national scale! At that time, customer satisfaction surveys weren't being done. I took the concept of homemakers making calls to a larger scale. I paid homemakers 40 cents for each completed call they made and charged the client 85 cents for written reports. That's how Direct Opinions started: with zero clients and one idea. In 1990, when I sold the company, it had over 225 employees making 2 million calls a year in nine cities.

Now for the technique for under $1. Here's how I got this idea. Years ago, Newsweek mailed me an offer for the busy executive who's too busy to read their magazine: I could get Newsweek on cassette tape. They certainly sent this offer to the wrong guy! First of all, I'm not *that* busy, and second, I enjoy looking at the pictures. I got a free tape, I listened to it, and I threw it on a corner of my desk.

One day, I had three prospects who would not return my phone calls. I knew that every one of these prospects was interested in my service *and* needed it, but I couldn't get one of them to call me back. One was a Cadillac dealer, the second was a high-end audio retailer, and the third was a major hospital.

Here's what I did.

I got a #10 business envelope, plain white, with no return address. I put a stamp on it—no postage meter, I handwrote the address, and I marked the envelope "personal". In it I put a cassette tape and a plain sheet of note paper with, "Please play this cassette tape in your car on your way home from work." I did not sign it. What would *you* do if you got a cassette like that?

On the tape I put this message:

"Hi, Mr. Jones. This tape will take just two minutes. I've got 1 minute and 57 seconds left. This is Hal Becker from Direct Opinions. The last time I spoke to you, you told me you were interested and that I should get back in touch with you, but you're hard to reach. I want to tell you the benefits of my program... (price, etc). Please drive carefully—are you wearing your safety belt? I'll call you Friday morning at 10:30."

What would you do if you heard a tape like that? The Cadillac dealer called me for an appointment. When I was walking through, I heard people whispering, "There's the idiot who sent the tape." Idiot? hardly. I've had the Cadillac dealer as a client for more than nine years.

The administrator of the medical center gave me an appointment. That office was one of the most beautiful I've ever seen. They didn't become my client, but they did answer my questions, and I got some great decorating ideas.

The audio retailer put a message on the other side of my tape saying they didn't want my services. If I call, the owner will remember me. I accomplished what I was trying to do.

This does work. And a few people at my seminars say they or someone else in their company received such a tape.

The thing is to be creative. Be an artist! With a big client, be more creative. For instance, you might want to send a telegram or an Eastern Onion. Do something.

Ruth Miller heads Cleveland's Tower City, one of the largest urban malls in the world. In wooing an international retailer to be a tenant, her people found out that the decision-maker collected toy wooden planes from all over the world. So Ruth Miller found a rare plane and sent it to that person.

Whatever you do, you want to get the point across in a way that gets your prospect's attention. Figure out what it will take to get the two of you together. You need to be creative, to be different from everyone else out there. When you read this, it might work to send a cassette tape, or it might not.

Customer Care

Point 1. To your customers, the company is you and everyone in it.

Think about your business. Basically, you do the same things as your competitors. What makes you different is *you*. And by *you*, I mean everyone, from the receptionist to the salesperson to the technical support or the people in the plant. It all boils down to everyone working together.

As a salesperson, you need to have a good reputation with your customer *and* with everyone in your company. If you have a reputation as being slick or something of a con artist, just pushing things through to get the sale, then you're not going to have a good relationship with support staff or with the customer.

It takes trust, and every salesperson needs to build trust with the rest of the staff in the company. Everyone in every area must constantly be trying to do what's best for the customer. That's how it has to be.

Your customer wants to be taken care of.

Remember the programmer who came to my rescue when my computer crashed? What I know and remember about that company is that on one of the worst days of my life, when my system crashed, they were on my doorstep within an hour.

Point 2. Pray for problems. They give you the opportunity to be a hero.

When I owned Direct Opinions, I *looked* for problems. Today, if I were to conduct a seminar for you and you were a little disappointed about something, I would need to talk to you and find out what it is. Then I would need to do whatever the situation calls for. Maybe I need to call someone and set matters straight. Maybe I need to go the library and check out a fact. Whatever is needed, I go above and beyond the call of duty, more than you expected me to do. What's going to happen? When you have a problem in the future and you call me, it won't be a problem.

You recognize it when someone goes above and beyond the call of duty. I recently bought a new television set, and the first time I plugged it in, it died. Poof! When I called the company, I expected them to say, "Bring it back in and we'll put it through service." Instead, they said, "We'll be out in one hour with a new set for you." Was I surprised! That tells me when I need service, they'll send someone right out.

Point 3. What to do when your contact keeps changing.

How many of your customers are companies which keep changing their agents or decision-makers? You have to start the relationship all over again, and again. Imagine starting that relationship off on the offense instead of on the defense. Here's how to do it:

You: "Hello, Ms. New. I want to come in so I can give

you a copy of everything that involves Revolving Doors, Inc. and Direct Opinions. I'll explain it briefly and answer any questions you might have."

Notice that I'm just letting the new person know what my company is all about. I'm not selling anything. I'm just saying, "We're here for you." Is the company impressed? You bet. The new person sees the difference between you and everyone else, that you do more for your customers than anyone else.

How to become a hero.

There are several ways to become a hero in your customer's eyes. The first way is to develop a positive attitude about objections and problems.

You *want* objections. You *want* problems. Without them you can't be better than anyone else.

You can realistically expect to be better than a dozen other competitors. Better yet, you can *easily* be better than all those competitors—*if* you have the right attitude and everyone in your company works together as a team.

Erase the words "No" and "I don't know" from your vocabulary. Instead, say "Yes." or "I'll get back to you by noon (or another specific time)."

If you say, "I don't have the answer now, but I'll research it and get back to you in a couple hours," what should you do if those couple of hours go by and you still don't have the answer?

Call back and say, "I don't have your answer yet, but I'll call you back by the end of the day (or whenever)."

If you say, "I'll give you a call so we can do lunch some time," then stay in touch. Make that call. Keep your word.

> *An earth-shattering fact: All you have to do is keep your word.*

Point 4. It's 4:45 on a Friday afternoon.

How often does this happen to you: It's just 15 minutes to the weekend and a customer calls and says, "I need a copy of that contract we just signed." The typical salesperson will say, "Okay, I'll get it to you on Monday."

I would say, "I can't come tonight, but I'll be near your company tomorrow. How about if I drop it off then?" What are they going to say at that point? "No, that's okay, drop it off Monday." If I drop it off on Saturday, will they be impressed?

Learn from the leaders in customer care

Isn't this one of your pet peeves? You're in a restaurant, the experience has been less than wonderful, and your waiter asks, "How was everything?" and then does *nothing* about it.

Compare that to the Cooker's restaurant chain: the food is okay, but the service is spectacular. They will do everything they can to make you happy.

One time four of us went there and the food was fine but the service was terrible. As usual, the manager came by and asked, "How's everything?" I told her, "The food was fine, but I think our waiter was absent the day you had customer service training." There was *no* bill, and each of us got a $10 gift certificate. We said we got paid $40 to eat there.

Another time, eight of us had brunch at the Ritz Carlton Hotel, a benchmark company famous for its service. A woman in our group didn't get the coffee she ordered. She saw the waiter was busy, and the coffee station was just a few feet away. She didn't think anything about it, she just walked over and poured herself a cup of coffee.

At the end of the meal I asked the waiter for the

check. He said, "There will be no bill." I was amazed. "What do you mean, no bill?" He said, "We're sorry for the inconvenience, sir." I couldn't imagine what he was talking about. "We're sorry the lady had to get her own coffee."

Now, we're talking about $80. I insisted, "It's no big thing," but the waiter said, "No, sir, that's our policy. I told him, "You're going to get a big tip." As he started to walk away, I called him back. "By any chance, are you working dinner tonight?"

As you can imagine, my friends love to go out to dinner with me.

Point 5. When customers don't know what they want.

Often customers don't know what they want. You have to help them figure it out.

To demonstrate this, let's replay another scenario with your car. When you take it in to have the oil changed, did they ask you a few questions? The service department probably gave you exactly what you asked for and no more. Instead, this could have happened:

You: "Please change the oil."

Hal: "Mind if I ask you a few questions?"

You: "Go ahead."

Hal: "When was the last time you had your car aligned?"

You: "Maybe six months ago. I don't really recall exactly when."

Hal: "Have you hit any chuckholes lately?"

You: "Are you kidding? At least once a week."

Hal: "Does your car go perfectly straight, or does it veer a bit?"

You: "A little bit."

Hal: "My guess is that you don't want to change your tires, that you want to keep them as long as you can, right?"

You: "At $75 a tire, you bet I do!"

Hal: "Are you aware that if you don't rotate them every 7,000 miles, your tires will wear unevenly and you'll have to buy two new tires? And you may have to throw two good tires out because you have to buy four tires at the same time?"

You: "I've got lots of other places to put that money."

Hal: "Do you want us to rotate the tires and align the car? It costs $8 to rotate the tires and $39 for the alignment."

You: "Of course! Do it."

Point 6. Take care of your customers: The satisfied ones and the dissatisfied ones.

There are two types of customers. (There are *always* two types of *any*thing.) Satisfied customers and dissatisfied ones. The key is that you have to *ask* your customer questions to find out what your customers want *and* if they're satisfied. Because guess what: if you have a customer, you have to *keep* that customer.

Think about the satisfied customer for a moment. You want the customer to wind up with a strong positive feeling. After all, most of us don't want to spend money.

If you've bought a car in the past two years, you can relate to this fact. You go to the dealership and get instant sticker shock. A new car sure is expensive; in fact, it's more than you planned to spend, more than you want to spend. You may even question whether you *should* spend that much.

But you spent it. And now, as you drive away from the dealership, you think, "I really spent a lot of money." What do you do next?

You sniff the new-car smell. You turn up the stereo. What are you doing? You're selling yourself on how great the car is. If the salesperson had done a good job, you would have felt comfortable with your decision, and you wouldn't have to be telling yourself you did the right thing.

It's easy to outshine the competition.

You can find lots of opportunities to be better than anyone else. The sad truth is that sales and service are *so poor* today that it is *really easy* to be the best.

You have all kinds of opportunities. They can seem trivial, but they give you a chance to show your customer what you can do.

Point 7. How to make your customer comfortable with the decision to buy.

You want the customer to leave with a strong positive feeling. Here are some ways to offer positive reinforcement:

- Sum up the customer's comments in a positive manner.

Both the salesperson and support staff should be doing this. Your support or technical person could say:

"You know, that (buying decision) really was a good move for you. We're really glad you decided to go with our system."

And this:

"I hope you're happy with this system. If you're ever

not happy about any aspect of it, call me!"

Your company is reinforcing the customer's decision from all angles.

- Be *sincere* when you reinforce the customer's decision.
- Tell the customer, "Our company is pleased with your support, and we hope you'll use our service again."
- Show enthusiasm for your product or service.

Notice how that word, enthusiasm, keeps popping up. Encourage the customer to use your services again, to call you with any little problem. Make the customer feel comfortable.

By the way, it's important that you have two-way communication with all your customers. That's the only way you'll know whether they're happy. And if they're not happy with the product, they'll be unhappy with you.

Point 8. Protect your reputation.

If you ever compromise your reputation, you'll never have the customer again. I tell people that even Mother Theresa could not save her reputation if she were ever caught shoplifting. Your reputation is all you have, so don't ever compromise it! No sale is that important!

Never close a door behind you, especially if you are in sales. If you develop a reputation at one company as a top salesperson and then go to another firm, you will keep your reputation, and you will find that your old customers still want to talk to you and deal with you. Because people buy from *people*.

A good reputation requires that you do what you say. If you tell someone you will call at a certain time, do it.

Period! No excuses. No ifs, ands, or buts.

Point 9. The guy in the glass.

This poem says it all about honesty.

The Guy in the Glass

By Cleo Ludwig, or so I'm told.

When you get what you want and you struggle for self,
   The world makes you king for a day.
When you go to the mirror, look at yourself,
   And see what that guy has to say.
He's the fellow to please, never mind all the rest,
   For he's with you clear to the end.
And you pass your most dangerous difficult test
   If the guy in the glass is your friend.
For it isn't your father, mother, or wife
   Whose judgment upon you is passed.
The fellow who counts more in your life
   Is the guy staring back from the glass.
May he be like Jack Horner and pull out a plum
   And think you're a wonderful guy,
But if the man in the glass says "Hey, you're only a bum,"
   Then you can't look him straight in the eye.
You may fool the whole world on the pathway of years,
   And get pats on the back as you pass.
But your final reward will be heartaches and tears
   If you cheated the guy in the glass.

Point 10. The dissatisfied customer.

If you stop to think about it, you will see that a dissatisfied customer wants to be a satisfied one. You can help make that happen. Best of all, you can be a hero.

While listening to a customer who is dissatisfied with the product or service received, you must remain calm and keep an open mind. Remember: the customer is not criticizing you personally. The customer is unhappy with the situation or product, not with you.

Just listen and say, "I'm here to help you."

- **Be sure you understand** why the customer is dissatisfied.
- **Note the reason for dissatisfaction,** so action can be taken. How do recalls happen? You don't know there's a problem with your product until you hear it from your customers. If you don't hear it, they'll be unhappy with *you*. They'll walk away. They'll tell everyone. So it's important that you have two-way communication.
- **Show empathy** for the customer.
- **Thank the customer** for taking the time to tell you about the problem. Some customers are intimidated about calling a company for a service problem. You want to let them know that you want to hear from them when they have a problem.
- **Never promise** to correct the mistake unless and until you're 100% sure you can deliver. Otherwise you run into this type of situation: Your customer calls to say he needs a Herculator right away. You say, "Sure thing. We'll get a Herculator out to you tomorrow morning." Then you call the warehouse and discover there's nary a Herculator to be found anywhere in the U.S. You have to order one from Asia. Now you have the awkward and unpleasant task of delivering this news to your customer. How much better if you had said to your customer, "Let me check out the Herculator situation. I'll get back to you within the hour."

Never make promises unless you're 100% sure you
can deliver!

- **Remain positive and enthusiastic** while the
customer is stating the dissatisfaction. Don't
become anxious or upset, as if you've never heard
this before. What if you go to your doctor and say,
"Doc, I have a pain in my chest," and the doctor
exclaims, "What?" and leaves the room. Does that
inspire confidence? Personally, I'd follow him,
because if he consults with a book or another doctor, I'm going elsewhere!

- **If the customer becomes hostile,** you still
must remain calm. Do not raise your voice. Do not
retaliate. If you punched me and I hit you back,
we'd soon be fighting. But if I *don't* punch you
back, it will be hard for you to fight with me. Have
you ever been in a relationship with someone who
doesn't argue back? Isn't it hard to argue with yourself? Remind yourself it's hard for people to fight
with someone who won't fight back.

Point 11. The nicest thing about the '90's is it's so easy to be the best.

Hal: "Hi, Bob. This is Hal Becker. I understand that
you're making decisions about Smurfometrics. I just
wanted to call and see if everything is okay. I'd like to
come in and meet you some time."

Bob: "I'm glad you called, because I need a copy of a
contract."

This is where most salespeople would say, "I'll see
you next week." This is where you have an opportunity
to be better than anyone else, to do more than the
competition. I'd have that contract on his desk the

same afternoon.

Believe me, from a salesperson's perspective, the nicest thing about the '80's and '90's is that *all* you have to do is be conscientious and keep your word, and you'll be doing more than anyone else. *Which is really easy.*

Don't you get bad service more often than you get good service? Isn't great service almost the exception? This is true no matter where you go and what you buy.

In selling, we talk about customer satisfaction and customer service. Let me tell you a little secret:

They're the same thing.

Customer satisfaction has been a buzz phrase in the '80's and '90's. Like a lot of other buzz phrases, it's meaningless. All it means is that once you get a client, you should keep that client.

How do you keep clients? Be conscientious Do more for them. Be sincere. Treat them the way you want to be treated.

Point 12. You have more dissatisfied customers than you realize!

The truth is that most dissatisfied customers do not complain. On the average, a business hears from only four per cent of its unhappy customers. This means that for every complaint a company hears about, another 26 customers have problems, and at least six of those problems are serious.

Most noncomplainers—between 65% and 90%—will not buy from you again. You will never know why. They will just evaporate!

You can, however, win back most customers who complain— between 54% and 70%—by resolving their complaints. Best of all, practically every one of these customers—up to 95%—will become loyal again if you handle their complaints well and quickly.

Keep these other two facts in mind: a satisfied customer will, on average, tell five other people; a dissatisfied customer will, on average, tell nine or ten other people, maybe as many as 20 people or more.

For more details, I encourage you to contact the Direct Selling Education Foundation in Washington, D.C., for its leaflet "Customers Mean Business" and the Department of Commerce (also in Washington, D.C.) for guides on this subject, including "Managing Consumer Complaints."

Point 13. Smarter? No. Angrier? Yes!

A recent article in my local newspaper claimed that customers are getting smarter. I disagree. Customers are getting angrier. I can prove it.

Take a piece of paper and a pencil, and jot down every day of the past week. Then, starting with yesterday and working your way backward, write down a poor experience you had that day. It might have involved a retail store, a restaurant, a service business. It might have happened in the store or on the phone.

I'll bet you can recall a bad experience every day of the week, because people just don't care. That's a shame. That's our society.

Point 14. A week in the life of a customer.

Is service really at such low ebb? Do companies lose that much in sales? The sad truth is that you can find examples of terrible service wherever you look—literally every day of the week!

Here's what happened in one week of my life:

Wednesday: I went to a travel agent—someone new a friend referred me to. I told her, "My plans fell through. I want to go anywhere in the world for one week, somewhere I can have fun and not think." She gave me a book and said, "Read through this." I said, "Give me five choices." She rattled off a list of every city in the world. So I went to my own travel agent, who gave me three choices—just what I wanted. I took her first recommendation.

Thursday: I got a lab bill for an emergency room visit. That really had me steamed because I'd been told the total cost would be $80, and here was a bill for another $56. When I called, the woman said, "We forget to tell people that sometimes this happens."

Friday: I had to buy running shorts for my vacation. At the first store there were no clerks in sight, and all the sizes were mixed together on one rack. I got mad and left. At the second store the clerk said the shorts were in the back. He disappeared. After 10 minutes, I left. The people at the third store were great but didn't have shorts. I found what I needed at the fourth store.

Saturday: I was in an upscale department store and saw a beautiful leather jacket for $600. Now, I usually shop at Value City, but this was a good month, and I said, why not? The jackets were all chained together. It took me five minutes to find a clerk who didn't have the key, didn't know where it was, and couldn't find it. I left.

Sunday: I didn't go out. I had 15 friends over to watch the game. I ordered five pizzas, but when I got there they had no record of the order. They finally found it half an hour later, and then they only made four pizzas. I left without the pizzas.

Monday: I needed customized software from the computer store. It was a $1,000 sale, but the salesman didn't know the product, didn't know the price, and didn't even know if the program was loaded. I walked out.

Tuesday: So far everything has gone fine. But I haven't been to dinner yet!

Customer care

The most important aspect of sales is going out and getting the customer. The second aspect is keeping them.

Think back to your last party. When it was over, who called you and thanked you for a good time? Didn't that make you feel good?

If you call the customer the day after he or she places and order, and you say, "I really appreciate you having trust and faith in me to deliver the order," isn't that the same thing? It hits home. Again, common sense.

Call back afterward, and say thank you. Remember: People buy from people. Your clients are buying you first and your products or services second.

Point 15. Reputation: Its all you've got.

All you've got is your reputation. Nothing else. So never, ever, compromise your reputation to make a sale. An example:

I was in a car dealership when a woman came in to have the body side trims, those little strips, glued back on her car. She asked the service manager how much it would cost, and he said $11. I was still there when she came back. The bill was $21.

She: "Excuse me, but you made a mistake. You said it cost $11."

He: "Oh, no, I'm sorry, I misquoted. It's $21."

The bottom line was that the dealership got $21—but at what a price. Will she ever go back? What will she tell everyone about that dealership?

Have you ever done anything like that in your company? The point is: don't. If you have to lose money, do it.

If you go out to the customer and you don't fulfill your promises, your company looks bad. You have to work as a team. Your reputation is important.

I recommend you visit your clients as much as possible. Write down the date and what happened. Keep highly organized notes.

Point 16. How about dessert? Add-on sales.

What happens when you go to McDonald's and order a cheeseberger, fries, and soft drink? They always ask, "What do you want for dessert?" Why do they do this? Because one out of five people will say yes.

Most stations in the quick-lube industry change your oil for $19. They certainly don't make any money on that. But one out of five people buy air cleaners and all that kind of stuff, and that raises the average sale enough so the company can make money.

I'm chairman of an organization called the Cancer Hotline, and we do a lot of fund raisers. One time I got all the concessions. I asked every person who ordered a hot dog or hamburger if they'd like chips or pop, and three out of ten said yes. That's 30% more, just because I asked. So it does work.

I saw a great example of this at a discount house.

The woman at the checkout counter asked the guy ahead of me, "Did you find everything you needed?" What a great idea. The customer said, "No, I couldn't find car batteries." The cashier grabbed the microphone and yelled, "Automotive!"

The only problem with this is that the line backed up. Imagine how great it would have been if the cashier had a pause button so she could take care of the next person in the meantime. I've never seen a store that had this, and I can't believe someone hasn't invented it yet. It would be so much more productive, because so many people walk out when checkout lines get backed up. You can take the idea—I don't want to do it. Consider it a bonus for reading carefully.

Who should follow up?

All of us, when we buy something, want to be able to count on it and on someone. Who should follow up? Company policies vary. If the salesperson has a relationship with the customer, the salesperson should follow up. Sometimes someone in the technical end is better. It should be the person most familiar with that account and with what's going on. Sometimes follow-up calls can be made by a third party, like Direct Opinions.

Regardless who follows up, the important thing is that the follow-up take place and that the customer feel comfortable. That's the bottom line—and yours.

A Case In Point

Point 1. What does the customer want?
Lets look again at the car dealership
on your corner.

So often I hear a salesperson or manager complain, "We show customers the benefits, and they get it cheaper somewhere else."

Why would a customer go elsewhere and buy a cheaper product? There are two reasons. Either there's a big difference in price, *or* there's a big difference in the salesperson's attitude. I see proof of this in every seminar:

Hal: "What kind of car do you drive?"

Joe: "A Hyundai Excel."

Hal: "How many dealers did you go to before you bought your Excel?"

Joe: "Three."

Hal: "Why did you buy it from the third dealer?"

Joe: "I got a good price."

Hal: "How far is the dealer from you?"

Joe: "About 25 miles away."

Hal: "Where's the closest dealer to you?"

Joe: "One mile."

Hal: "Did you have a trade-in?"

Joe: "No."

Hal: "How far apart were the prices?"

Joe: "Less than $100."

Hal: "So why didn't you buy the Excel from the dealer who's practically on the corner of your street?"

Joe "The salesperson was a jerk, an idiot!"

Hal: "Let me guess: the salesperson jerked you around on the price. Am I correct?"

Joe: "Yes."

That is scary.

As I've already said, every dealer in the country pays the exact same price for the car. Let's assume that both of the dealerships Joe went to have good service departments. And when the deal is done, the prices are within $100 of each other—which happens 90% of the time.

Joe went to the salesperson he liked and trusted most. The dealer on Joe's corner could have—*should have*—made the sale.

This is the kind of situation I would be absolutely furious about if I owned the dealership on the corner. Why? Because Joe's the kind of person who will want to bring his car in for service.

I prove this point in every seminar by asking for a show of hands: How many of you want a good price on your car? *everyone.*

Now imagine if the salesperson says to you:

"I just want to make sure this is the car you want. I promise you the price will be competitive. Go to two other dealers (on the average, car buyers go to three dealers—statistically, 2.7 dealers—because the buyers don't trust the dealer), and if you get a price within $100 of my price, we'll make a deal that's comfortable for you."

"Whatever that price is, I'll add $175, because every time you bring your car in for service, I'll have a free loaner for you. Not a rattle-trap, but a car comparable to yours, clean and in perfect shape, to drive until your car is ready. And every time you pick up your car, it will be washed."

How many of you would pay the $175? *Three out of four people say yes.*

That means people want good service. So that's what dealerships want to sell.

Think about what this means! Car dealerships have created this situation where people are running around buying cars on the basis of the price tag, when what people *really want* is to be taken care of.

In the past two weeks two people asked me to recommend a good place to buy a car, in one case a Honda, and in the other case a Ford. I gave each person the name of a dealership, and they bought a car as fast as you can say, "Your loan is approved." Why? Because they trusted the owner and because it was a pleasant experience. But most people have unpleasant experiences.

Whether you look at that extra $175 from the buyer's viewpoint or the dealer's viewpoint, it's a fair deal, considering that people keep a car for three years on the average. With four service visits a year, and $15 for a loaner and $5 for a car wash, the total over three years would be $240. Everybody wins.

Do you know why most people don't go back to the dealer for service? They perceive that it's more expensive. But the truth is, the price is very competitive.

Here's why: First of all, every repair shop, whether it's at a dealership, a gas station, or wherever, uses Chilton's manual to set their technicians' hourly rate.

Second, and much more important—and what few people realize, today's cars have on average four to five times as many on-board computers, and every car manufacturer has its own specialized diagnostic equipment.

A Toyota dealership, for example, uses diagnostic equipment designed for Toyota cars. Do you think the gas station can invest in a whole roomful of computerized equipment for all the different car manufacturers?

Now, when you have a physical problem bothering you, where do you go? If it's a heart problem, you go to a cardiologist. So why do you take your car to the corner gas station? I want to take my car to the people who see that make and its problems every day.

And third, if you follow your maintenance schedule and wash your car on a weekly basis, guess what will happen? You'll have a car that will last just about as long as you want it to. And if you go to the dealer with a problem and it isn't fixed properly, guess who backs you up now: the dealer and the manufacturer—in effect, you have an insurance policy.

Think about how the car sales and service system works and what customers *really* want. And think about your product or service.

10

Goal Setting and time Management

You've heard it before, but it's true, true, true: **A goal without a plan is only a wish.**

Most people wish for things to happen. They don't *plan* for things to happen. You have to plan things. Period. You have to plan how you're going to get there, wherever *there* is: to get married, to buy a house, to get the job, to increase sales by 40%, to get an answer from a prospect who never returns your call.

The plan sets you apart from the competition, from the rest of the world.

Point 1. Goals: Your rudder.

Goals are a must. Without goals, you have no direction for your time management. Goals can be defined as what is truly needed and wanted. First, consider your own needs and wants within the organization, so you can get personal satisfaction; and second, the organization's needs and wants, so you achieve what the boss considers important.

Look at your sales-call goal. Could you make ten calls a day? Are you too busy to do that? Are you doing really well? Are you very happy with the income you are producing?

If you'd like to do better, then the only way to do that is to sell more, and the only way to do that is to get more prospects.

You will be surprised how much more work you can get done on a given day when you manage your time effectively. If this is an area where you could improve a lot, there are many books and seminars. Look at the best salespeople you know: they are not frazzled; they are highly organized.

If I could teach you a way to be unbelievably successful working only half-days, would you be interested? Yes? Okay, which do you prefer to work: the first 12 hours or the second 12 hours? That reminds me of what Stephen Leacock, the Canadian humorist said:

"I'm a great believer in luck.

The harder I work, the luckier I get."

Without going into time management in great detail, let me give you some key ideas.

You can find a lot of ways to make shortcuts. You can streamline a lot of your client calls.

You want to get the most results out of your working day. If you start work at 8 a.m. and work until 6 p.m., you are putting in long hours.

And you most likely have other things in your life that are more important than your job. Your family comes first, and that's the way it should be.

I find there are other times when I can do things. For instance, I didn't do quotes or proposals during the day. I did them at night, when I was watching television.

You have to study your own day. What are you doing? What paperwork is necessary? Every office has paperwork. Some salespersons spend 50% of their time on sales and 50% on paperwork. That's not very productive, is it? Use a daily planner to see where your time actually goes. If something in your office work is *not* efficient, you have to sit down and figure out what the problem is and how to solve it.

If you can increase the time you spend in front of decision- makers by 20%, you can increase your income and your company's by 20%. If you can find just 15 more minutes in each day to get in front of a decision-maker, that totals an hour and a half in a week, which is the equivalent of working an extra day every week!

We all have habits. Make sure your habits are productive for *you*. Some people work out at 6 a.m. Other people work out at 6 p.m. What works for the early birds would never work for the night owls and vice versa.

If something works well for you, leave it alone, don't change it. Just become as productive as you can while enjoying yourself.

Point 2. Two ways to save time on proposals:
First, remember K.I.S.S.

A lot of times, when salespersons prepare a proposal, they include everything but the kitchen sink. What's the result? When the customer looks at the proposal, it's too much to absorb, and if the customer has to present the proposal to someone else in the company, it's too hard to do right.

Think about the junk mail you get. Don't you read what's quick and throw out what's thick? The same thing is true of proposals.

My message is simple. Ask yourself:

How simple can I make this proposal?

K.I.S.S. Keep It Simple, Stupid.

Over the years I've found that the shorter my quotes are, and the more concise, the more business I get.

This can make *your* life easier—*and* more profitable.

A second timesaver on preparing proposals:

Here's another way to save time. For less than $200 you can have your proposals done in no time.

Make up one major proposal that covers all the different types of benefits and services your company can provide. Give each item a different letter: benefit A, benefit B, and so on. Put it in the word processor, and when you have a proposal, all you have to do is select the parts you want and put them into your proposal, instead of writing that proposal from scratch. You make one investment of time, and the job is basically done.

Point 3. Setting goals.

Keep in mind that every goal must meet four criteria:
1. It has a specific time frame (days, weeks, or months).
2. It is measurable (so you know when you've achieved it).
3. It is realistic (so you don't get frustrated and give up).
4. It is challenging (so you have a sense of accomplishment). You can apply these criteria to your personal goals as well. Maybe you want to buy a house, put money aside for your kids' education. Whatever your goal, it boils down to the same thing.

Let's say my average sale is $1,000 and that my goal is to make $10,000 more in the coming year. This is not my company's quota. It's the goal I set for myself.

To get this $10,000, I need 10 new clients. I know

that if I make 500 cold calls, 25 of those prospects will be interested and that 10 will buy and will become my new clients.

So I need to make 500 cold calls. Figuring on 200 workdays in a year, I would need to make 2.5 additional cold calls a day. This is how to determine what it will take to reach a sales goal.

It's just like working out. You have to set your goals and then carry them out if you want to actually achieve them. How many people actually work out 3 or 4 times a week to get the great body they want? Very few!

Most people are weak. They take the course of least resistance. The only way to reach your goal is to break it down into bite-size pieces. You do a little bit every day. That's how anything gets done, including the biggest jobs.

If you don't translate your quota into a daily plan, then what are you doing a few days before the end of the month? After the 25th of the month you find salespersons scrambling and making frantic calls to meet the company's quota.

Why do the top salespeople always go over the company quota? Because they are working harder than everyone else and are working consistently to meet their own goals.

To be outstanding, you say:

Here's what I have to do *every day.*

Not every year, *not* every quarter,

Not every month, but every *day.*

The same holds true in areas other than sales, such as response time. Does your company have real hard numbers on response time? Every medium-size or big service company I know that's productive rates its response time. A good goal in most cases is six hours, and in successful service companies every call is tracked, monitored, and rated.

If I were manager of customer service, that would be very important. I would constantly try to cut my response time to less than six hours, and I would publicize my policy and record to my customers. That's my opinion.

Point 4. Manage your time if you want to succeed. Make planning a daily habit.

We develop habits because that's the only way to get anything done. Then we get so used to our own habits that it takes work to change them.

Fold your arms across your chest. Now switch hem—fold them the opposite way. You have to think about what you're doing, don't you? If every time you folded your arms, you had to do it this opposite way, it would be difficult and would take some time to get used to.

Life is like that. The only way to change your habits is to try new things and to practice them even when they are uncomfortable.

The greatest time management course out there is "Time and Territory Management" by—who else?—Xerox. They still have the best courses. This is a three-day course. Actually, it's one-half day of training and two and one-half days of repetition and more repetition so that you absorb the material.

(Any course you find, whether it's a memory course, a listening course, or whatever, will be like that. The only way to get better is by practice and repetition.)

This course is spread over a two-week period. On the wall they have a huge daily planner: a master grid broken into time increments, with space for everyone's name and everyone's day. In this course you see for yourself exactly where your time goes and how much you lose.

Everyone in this course, regardless of what type of company he or she works for, spends on average the same amount of time in front of decision-makers: it's one and one-half hours a day for people in outside sales, and three hours a day for people in retail.

Keep track of your time for the next week—every 15 minutes of every day. You'll be surprised to see where your time really goes.

We all waste time. Unless and until I sit down with you, I don't know how much more efficient *you* could be. But *you* can sit down and figure out how much time you actually have left. Maybe you are already as efficient as you can possibly be. Maybe you're super-busy, but you've got to find a way to find more time for sales or another priority. Or maybe you find you have so many hours, and here's how you're going to put them to better use.

Waiting at lights.

You probably drive at least 12,000 miles a year. We all deal with a lot of traffic. One day I got so tired of waiting for traffic lights that I took a stopwatch with me and timed how long I spent waiting for lights to change. Considering all the time I spend on highways, I was amazed to discover that I spent 24 minutes a day waiting for lights to change. That comes to 144 hours a year—more than in a two-week vacation! If I work 50 years, I will have spent 2.5 years of my life waiting for the light to change. You can see why cellular car phones are so popular and so useful.

Point 5. If you don't already have a daily planner, get one. That five dollars will change your life!

When you tackle the process of changing your habits, the most important tool is a daily planner or calendar. There are all kinds of brands and types and sizes. The important thing is to pick the kind suited to your needs and to be sure it has a page for each day—and then use it. This works!

You need a daily planner to block out time to meet your goals. You also need it to remember things.

Look at what you do every day. How many times are you sitting at your desk and your spouse calls and wants you to do something. Hours later, you're driving home, whistling away, and you suddenly realize you forgot it? You're dead meat! Or how often, when a customer calls and asks for something, do you say you'll get right back to her—and then you forget?

Why did you forget? Of course! You forgot to write it down. You need a list! With a to-do list, you won't forget. Otherwise it's like going to the supermarket: either you'll forget the one thing you really need, or you'll wind up with 32 rolls of toilet paper.

Another thing happens when you start writing things down. You don't waste mental energy trying to remember.

When someone asks me what I did Friday, or what I have to do tomorrow, all I have to do is look at my list. It takes the pressure off. When you really start to use a daily planner, you live by it. If I ever lost my daily planner, I would sit in the middle of the room and cry. My whole life is in that little book.

When you've made your list, prioritize it. Things marked "A" have to be done today. With "B" items, if I don't get to them today, I have to do them tomorrow. "C" items can wait, even until next week. And "D" items can be done whenever I get around to them, if ever.

This is how to set your goals, how to plan. Maybe this sounds too basic to you, or too much like plain common sense. Well, I don't know of anyone I have *ever* met—and I don't usually use words like *ever*—who has tried a daily planner and has quit using it.

Get a planner you can carry everywhere. Whatever size it is, it should be something you won't lose, and it should have enough space to write everything you need. Maybe you want a planner small enough so you always have it on you. Maybe you want a big planner so you can't lose it and so you can put everything in it. Whatever you get, use it. *Write things down.*

You cannot be too organized. Being organized is the only way to be in business. If you have a sales territory, it is your business. If you provide technical support, it is your business.

You know in your mind what you want to do. Write it down, do it, and scratch it off your list.

Keep in mind where and when you do your best thinking. Driving? In the shower? Just before you fall asleep? One guy told me, "In the creek." Apparently that was his place of solitude.

Also, you can now get a small portable dictator for under $30. Try it. You'll find that it can help you do things that will make you more money.

I know a company where the president bought dictation machines for all the sales staff just so they won't lose an idea when they're on the road. I did a seminar for this company, and whenever I said something that struck someone, that person would walk off and dictate a comment that the company should work on that thing.

Point 6. How to plan your day.

The way you start your day is crucial. The first 15 minutes are the most important and set the tone for your day; your real task in the first 15 minutes is to plan your day.

Look at all the things undone from yesterday plus the things you need to do today. Make one central list so that you don't forget everything and so that you don't waste mental energy on working to remember everything.

If you see that your day will be very busy, you know that you'll have to keep phone calls and meetings short and that wherever possible you'll have to postpone responding to requests from other people. No matter how busy your day, be sure to allow one to two hours for crises—they always happen.

Then ask yourself a series of questions:
- How can I best make my plan work today?
- Who do I need to consult?
- Who can I talk with in order to prevent part of my plan from being sabotaged?
- Do I need quiet time to concentrate? How can I get it? When?
- Is my schedule so busy that I need to say *no* more often today?

When you *have* to do something, you'll make the time to do it. But you don't make time for things you don't want to do. If I don't want to go out and make cold calls today, but I want to go work out, guess what's going to happen.

Point 7. For just a buck or so, you can get highly organized.

Go buy a plastic box, 500 index cards, and dividers for January to December. For every sales call, staple that company's business card to the index card. Write down the date of the visit, what happened: what you said and what they said. Just a couple lines are enough.

Say, for example, that you just saw a new prospect who told you, "Call me back in three months." On the index card, write, "Ms. Jones said to give her a call in three months."

Now would a typical salesperson call back in three months? No. Your typical salesperson would forget about it. But you're not going to be a typical salesperson. Pull out your daily planner and say, "Three months...that will be December 20. How about if I give you a call on December 19 around 2 p.m. Would that be okay?"

What will the customer start doing? Exactly what the people in my seminars do. Laugh at me. But guess what happens. I call around December 20, and before the end of February, I've made the sale.

The same thing happens with accounts payable or receivable. If I know a client isn't going to call me back on the subject, I also know what's going to happen if I don't write a note to myself. I'll forget all about it until the computer spits out a major report.

A last word about goals and planning.

It cannot be emphasized enough: set goals and plan

daily, no matter how difficult it is at first. As you practice and pick up ideas from week to week, you will
become more and more proficient. Don't give up early
on; the first six weeks are the hardest. Here are three
words to remember:

   Discipline isn't fun.

   But to do well in anything, you have to discipline
yourself, and that takes time and hard work.

   That, in a nutshell, is a course on time management.
The key to bettering yourself is to change your habits.
Again, it's common sense. Except that common sense is
not at all common.

Point 8. Keep it all in perspective.

   Nine years ago I didn't feel so well. Some pulled muscles had been bothering me for a few months—I felt as
if I'd been kicked in the stomach. So I went to the doctor. He did some tests and he said, "Hal, get your affairs
in order and be in the hospital in two hours. You have
terminal cancer."

   That was not quite what I wanted to hear. Instead of
being handed a tube of Ben-Gay, I spent the next eight
months in the hospital undergoing chemotherapy. To
make a long story short, I shouldn't be alive. I lost 55
pounds, which meant I weighed about 88 pounds, and
I lost every hair on my body.

   Why do I tell you this? We think the world hinges
on whether we make the next sale, and we get all
worked up over trivial things. The little things are what
eat at us.

   Think back to the problems you had yesterday. How
many of them are gone? And even more of the problems you had last week or last month are gone today.

All the problems you have today will be gone, if not tomorrow, then next week or next month.

There is no one sale that will change your life if you make it or lose it. All of us will face a traumatic experience: a major illness or accident or the death of a loved one. *Those* experiences are the ones that make a difference in our lives.

So don't let the little things get to you. The key is to do the best you can all the time, on every project, and then get on to the next one.

My mentor, Sue Seidman, told me this:

>**The idea is 10%. The implementation is 90%.**

And she follows up by saying:

>**And you can't teach pigs to fly, no matter how long you make the runway.**

11

The Art of Closing

What is closing? It's obtaining a written or verbal contract. When do you close? A really successful salesperson almost knows instinctively when and how to close. The good news: this instinct can be learned.

How do *you* learn the closing instinct? You close soon, and you close often. Your own good judgment and common sense are the most important factors in deciding when and how to close.

You base your decision on the answers to two questions:

First: "Do I have all the information necessary to make a suitable recommendation on pricing and product?"

And second: "Have I been able to establish sufficient value and need in the customer's mind?"

What is a trial close? It's an "If I...then will you...?" proposition. The easiest way to define a trial close is to give a couple examples:

If I can show you a system that is very competitive in price and will do all the things that will make you more productive, *then* will you be interested?

If I can provide you a sales course that will show you how you can improve your confidence and skill, increase your sales, and have fun doing it, *then* would you be interested?

If the answer is *no,* it means the customer is not interested. If the answer is *yes,* the next step is to close the sale. That's a trial close.

Point 1. When should you close?

You should close any time and all the time. Remember what I said earlier: fully 63% of salespeople say they make the sales after the fifth rejection.

What does that mean? Most of the time, you'll have to hear no five times before you hear a yes. The top salespeople close a minimum of five times in one conversation.

And what do you do after you close? You shut up! Be quiet. You've asked a question. Wait for an answer!

You just got out of school, didn't you?

I'd been out of Xerox training school only three weeks, and I was wired. I went out to make sales calls. I did all the things they taught me: I knocked on doors, I asked questions, I closed.

So here I was facing this guy. I closed, I shut up, I looked at him. He looked at me. I kept looking at him, and he kept looking at me. A bead of sweat started down my forehead. I felt as two hours went by—I'd never spent a longer two minutes. Finally, I broke down and spoke:

Hal: "I'm doing something wrong here."

Him: "Hal, chill out. Eat some fiber. Let me ask you something: you've got my business card. You know where I work."

Hal: "Yes, this is your company."

Him: "And I've got *your* card. I know where *you* work. Correct?"

Hal: "Correct."

Him: "What you *don't* know is what I did before this."

Hal: "Okay, I'll bite. What did you do before?"

Him: "I used to be a sales manager for Xerox. You just got out of school, didn't you?"

Well, I wanted to die.

Point 2. So you don't die.

You don't want to die a thousand deaths. You want to be a killer. So let's spend a few minutes on the traits and actions of ineffectual closers.

- They're not sure when to close.
- They are inflexible. They have limited techniques.
- They have a fear of failure.
- They are not sure if they're going in the right direction.
- They are overanxious.
- They are afraid of being too pushy or too aggressive.
- They don't bring the customer to a logical business decision.
- They imply closings instead of stating them.
- They're afraid of confrontations.
- They stay in the conversation mode and don't move into the selling mode.
- They lack enthusiasm.
- They lack skills.

You will not be this kind of weenie! *You* will learn the skills you need, and you will be a confident, skilled closer.

I don't believe in spending time on negatives; I want to spend time on positives.

Point 3. Do you think it's harder than it is?

At this point I ask people attending my seminar which they think is harder:

Is it harder to close for an appointment—to call someone up, identify yourself, say you'd like to ask some questions, and then close for an appointment?

Or is it harder to close for an order—to be sitting in front of the customer, ask your questions, and then ask if the customer wants the product?

Anywhere from 40% to 60% of the salespersons I talk to think it's harder to close for the sale. I truly believe they imagine closing to be harder than it actually is, for this reason:

The customer knows your job is selling. The customer therefore *expects* you to ask for the order!

In my own opinion, and it's just my opinion, it's harder to ask for the appointment because I'm asking for a piece of their time. If I'm in front of them, they expect me to ask them to buy my product.

If I came to your house to talk to you about insurance, you'd be waiting for me to say, "Do you want it?" If I gave you a quote on replacing your roof, you'd be waiting for me to say, "Do you want it?"

Think about all the times you desperately want to buy something and be done with it, but first you have to make a dozen decisions.

I swear the most confusing thing you can do is to go into a store to buy a pair of jeans. You have to decide whether you want a straight cut, boot cut, navigator cut, or whatever cut. Do you want a zipper or button fly? a 501, 301, 201, or 101? Do you want acid wash, stone wash, or denim look?

Once you've decided all that and found a pair that really fits, you get to the counter, and what do you find? Another decision: cash or charge? You'd think they'd say, "Thank you, enjoy."

In my opinion, the customer expects the same thing. When you're in front of him, the customer is waiting for you to ask, "Do you want it?"

Point 4. Symptoms of unnecessary fear of closing.

When you ask for the order, which of these symptoms do you experience:

> sweaty palms,
>
> paralysis,
>
> shaking knees, or
>
> all of the above.?

The good news: these are all psychological things you can overcome. You can know your stuff: your product and the competition. And you can do your homework so that information is in your head, so it's always available when you need it.

Most important, you ask questions. Frankly, I think closing is not the big thing that so many people make it out to be. If I, as the salesperson, have asked you, the customer, all the questions I need to ask, then I know everything I need to know, I have led you along the path, and closing happens naturally.

People make such a big deal about closing because they have been *telling* instead of *asking,* and they haven't brought the customer and the situation to the point where a sale is the natural conclusion.

> *TELLING instead of ASKING is a habit. Break the habit of telling. Develop the habit of thinking in questions.*

Point 5. What makes a salesperson successful in closing?

Here are the traits of a successful closer. The successful salesperson has learned and does these things:

1. Knows when to close.
2. Skilled in variety of closing techniques.
3. Closes often, whenever there is an opening.
4. Displays high degree of enthusiasm.
5. Displays overt sense of confidence.
6. Is knowledgeable about products and competition.
7. Is perceptive and has good people skills; can read the customer.
8. Aware of buying signals.
9. Is skilled in minimizing objections.
10. Continually checks customer's level of understanding.
11. Continually seeks agreement on key issues.
12. Brings customer to logical business decision.
13. Does not go past the sale.
14. Listens effectively.
15. Is creative.
16. Can sell incentives effectively.
17. Does not get cocky or cute.
18. Makes a smooth transition from conversation to selling.
19. Is always professional.
20. Develops closing instinct.

Refer back to this list whenever you need to.

Point 6. Half the game is in watching.

Approach closing like a game. There are as many moves and strategies as there are people. The good news is that you can learn to close successfully by doing one thing:

Watch your customer.

Read your customer. See if he or she is interested. Where is he or she coming from?

In particular, watch the customer's eyes and smile. In most cases, the eyes and smile are the windows to a person's soul and will reveal almost everything.

True, there are a few exceptions. Some people are pathological liars, and it's hard to figure them out, but they represent a tiny percentage of the people you will deal with.

Don't get cocky or cute. Always be professional. If you're ever in front of a customer who starts to get real loose and do things out of place, like swearing a lot, do NOT behave likewise. Stay professional. All professionals do this. If you go to the dentist and say, "This *!@#$% tooth is killing me," you'll never hear your dentist say, "Yeah, I know what you mean, the same *!@#$% thing happened to the *!@#$% patient before you." Never!

View yourself as a doctor of sales.

Whenever you are selling something or fulfilling a customer's need, that customer wants someone who is knowledgeable about the product or service and who, as a bonus, is pleasant to be around.

The father of closing techniques.

The successful closing techniques of 50 years ago are still valid today. In my seminar manual I include, word for word, the techniques of J. Douglas Edwards, who was known as the grandfather of closing techniques.

Point 7. I took the manual off the shelf and made it a game.

Years ago, when I was first given these closes, guess what I did? I put them on the shelf. A few years later I decided, "Maybe they've got something here." I decided to look at closing from two angles.

First angle: If I don't look at this or read it, I'm not going to better myself.

Second angle: I looked at it like a chess game. (By the way, I don't play chess, even though I did buy an onyx chess set in Mexico—I didn't think Customs would let me go through without one.) Wouldn't it be fun to always be in control, to be one step ahead in a sales conversation, and to try different things with that customer and see what happens? It's fun to play that game.

So I decided to memorize these closes and to use different closes in different situations. I would ask myself, "Which of these closes should I use?"

One day while I was waiting in a lobby to see the decision- maker, I picked up my notepad and wrote down the close I would try that day. An amazing thing happened:

Selling became so much more fun. Because I made it fun.

You know from other areas of your life that if you just do the same thing all the time, it gets boring. *very* boring. If you do different things all the time, life is more fun. So do the same thing with closings.

Point 8. The order blank close.

This is the most fundamental of closes. You ask a question, and you fill in the answer on your order blank or contract— whatever your closing form is.

You don't ask, "Shall we go ahead?" You ask, "What

is the correct full name?" or "What is your delivery address?" As long as the prospect doesn't stop you, he or she has bought. You assume the prospect has bought.

When you've filled out the entire form, do *not* say, "Sign this." All our lives we've been warned to be careful, to beware when we sign something. Instead, say, "Would you okay this for me, please?"

Point 9. The alternative choice close.

This is simply: "Which do you prefer? Cash or credit?" Regular or decaf? A 13-inch screen or a 19-inch screen? Delivery on Friday or Monday? It's an either-or close.

Point 10. The free trial; a.k.a. "Puppy Close".

The free-trial close is called the puppy-dog close. If I dropped off a puppy at your house on Friday, for you to have just over the weekend, you—or someone in your family—would insist on keeping that puppy, even if it had destroyed your house in just that one weekend.

When color television sets were first introduced back in the late 1950's, retailers couldn't sell them. Almost the only shows in color were Disney, Bonanza, and Ed Sullivan.

Well, a guy named Dumont decided to use the puppy-dog close. On Friday he dropped color sets off at people's homes, and on Monday he returned to pick the sets up. This was back when families had two parents. The entire family was home Sunday night, and they gathered around the only television set in the house and watched it together. Guess what happened after the family had watched a show in color together on Sunday evening? They kept the color television sets.

You can apply this to technical and professional equipment. For example, most architects and designers have heard about CAD- CAM but don't have the system in their offices.

Ignore issues of price for a moment; why don't these people have CAD-CAM? They haven't learned how to use it. If it were my job to sell CAD-CAM's, I would put a system in their office, give them a one-week training program so they felt comfortable with the software, and then I'd let them use it for a few days.

Now are they going to want it? And if money is an objection, are they going to find a way to finance the purchase? You bet they will!

I've heard salespeople tell me that CAD-CAM systems are too complex, that systems have been put in and people can't use them, that customers get frustrated by how difficult the systems are.

My response is that people *have* learned how to deal with complex products. People have learned how to deal with computer hardware and software. It all hinges on whether you do *your* job.

Ask yourself whether you or someone else in your company takes one of the following approaches:

- Our product is so complicated that our customers don't have the intelligence or the education to run it.
- The product manual cannot be translated into plain English.
- We don't *want* to translate the product manual into plain English.
- We're too *busy* to translate the product manual into plain English.
- We've already tried it once (or ten years ago), and it

didn't work.
- Nobody else does it. Why should we?
- You can't compare our product to a color television set.

A similar set of reasons can also be given for not preparing an effective training system.

In my not-so-humble opinion, all the above reasons are excuses and *hogwash*.

Let's consider the example of copiers, a business product we're all familiar with. Let's say you want a copier.

Now, all copiers do basically the same thing: they make copies, they reduce, they sort, they can even get the paper to turn itself over under the lid so the machine can copy both sides. Nobody has anything really different on the market.

Salesperson Al brings in Brand A copier for your office to use on a trial basis. He drops it off, gives a brief demonstration, and vanishes. What happens? The copier jams, nobody in your office knows what to do, and you go back to using your old machine. Right?

When I come in with a copier, I spend time with you. I practically camp out in your office. I make sure you know how to use it, how to change the paper trays, how to unjam it. I make sure that, if—no, *when*—a problem comes up, you know how to reach me right away. And when you call, either I'll help you through the problem over the phone, or else I'll come out right away to resolve your problem and to stick with you until you're comfortable again with the machine.

Guess what you'll do? The decision-maker will ask the key operators, "What do you think?" and they'll say, "Let's buy Hal's machine." That's how I made my sales.

The same principles apply to complex equipment, such as CAD- CAM, which is computer-aided design or computer-aided manufacturing. I know designers who won't touch a CAD-CAM. The reason? They haven't been trained. If a salesperson made it easy for them, those designers wouldn't be able to live without the product!

The same thing is true of computers. If I go out and buy Lotus 1-2-3 and don't get training, will I use it? No! If I buy a Macintosh, with a menu that's so easily driven, and if someone spends a few minutes teaching me how to use it, am I going to start playing around with it? Yes. Am I going to find that I cannot live without buying it and using it? Absolutely!

It's true with any product or service no matter how complicated or how simple it is: if you have a *need* and if I can show you how I can meet that need, you will be sold.

Pique the prospect's interest. Demonstrate the *benefits*.

Once you capture interest, you will find that the customer has a thirst for more knowledge.

Point 11. The Ben Franklin close.

This close is useful when you have an indecisive customer and you just can't seem to uncover the real objection. It begins: "As you know, Ben Franklin was one of our wisest Americans. Whenever he was in the type of situation you're in today, he felt the way you do. If it was the right thing to do, he wanted to be sure to do it. And if it was the wrong thing, he wanted to be sure to avoid it.

"Here's what he would do. He would take a plain sheet of paper (you do that) and draw a line down the middle (you do that). At the top of the left column he wrote "YES" (write it), and at the top of the left column he wrote "NO" (write it). And he'd list all the reasons for and against his decision. Why don't we do that and see what happens?"

Now you spin the paper around to the customer, hand the customer your pen, and say, "Let's see how many reasons we can think of in favor of your decision today." You help the customer fill out that side. When you get to the negative side, say, "Let's see how many reasons you can think of against it." And you shut up.

The customer won't be able to think of more than a few. Then you add each side them up, and ask, "Well the answer is pretty obvious, isn't it?"

Point 12. The call back close.

If a customer were interested, he would have called you. So if you want to follow up, you have to think of a *relevant* but *new* benefit. You present that, then go back over the other benefits that were important to the customer, and close again.

Point 13. The lost sale close.

This is for the time you've done everything possible but have still failed. Maybe you've run out of steam or maybe the customer is furious. The one imperative is that you must use this in all honesty and sincerity.

You pack up and have one foot outside the door when you turn and say, "Pardon me, I wonder if you would help me for a moment. I really believe this product is right for you. I must have done something wrong. I know it's my fault, and I'm truly sorry. I really don't want to make this mistake again. Would you mind telling me what I did wrong?"

Now, if that customer needs your product and has the money to buy it, then you *did* indeed do something wrong, it IS your fault, and you *should* apologize. And it works.

If—and this is a huge if—you apologize with sincerity, you will find that this close will get you sales, because the customer will say, "It's not you, it's... ," and that will be the real objection.

Point 14. The "I'll think it over" close.

This close is one of my favorites. You've made your presentation, and the customer wants to sleep on the decision. You ask, "Just to clarify my thinking, exactly what phase of this do you want to think over? Is it this? Is it that? Is it that you don't like short balding guys?" The customer will say no to every question, which means the customer is saying yes to you. "Is-it" them to death. What you want to do is get down to the real objection so you can close the sale.

Point 15. The question close.

Use this when the customer asks a question such as, "Can I get it in green?" or "Do you have next-day delivery?" You respond with, "Do you want it in green?" or, "Do you want next-day delivery?" The customer who says yes has bought. Virtually every salesperson encounters situations like this every day.

Point 16. The similar situation close.

This technique works well at all points in sales presentations, and it's remarkably underused. When you go down a street, how many houses do you see with a sign for Security R Us?

A good salesperson, once he or she has sold to one homeowner, will go up and down the street, saying, "Mr. Smith, I'm with Security R Us. Your neighbors, the Joneses, just got our security system because they don't want to be robbed and pillaged again. Can we give you a quote?"

Let's say you just installed a computer system for Kicks and Associates. You go next door and say, "Hello, Ms. Johnson, I just installed a computer system for Kicks next door. Could I ask you a few questions about your firm?" What's she going to say? Most people want to keep up.

Ask your customers if you can use their name as referrals. The salesperson who's most impressive is the one who can say, "Here's our whole customer base. Call anybody." That's a whole different level of confidence: "Call any one of our customers."

I hate it when somebody gives me a list of four people to call. Remember this: most salespersons—including your competitors—will only hand out the names of three or four referrals.

Give referrals. People like to associate with people who are successful. There is no right or wrong way here. Typically, I usually suggest that if you can't give the prospect some names of people you'd like him to know or that he's familiar with, you might ask, "Would you like me to give you the names of architects (and so on)?" In other words, pick. Or let the prospect choose.

Point 17. Develop flexibility and variety.

Your selling efforts must be balanced. You must be able to thoroughly uncover customer needs through effective summaries and to close the customer for commitment, while creating the least degree of pressure, and while fostering a firm business relationship.

You *must* do two things in closing.

First, develop the flexibility to close for varying degrees of commitment. Close for a trial, for an order, for a proposal.

And second, develop a variety of techniques. Don't use just one close. Try many. Also use different techniques for different commitments. You might use one type of close when you go for a trial order, another type when you want an appointment, and another type for a close.

Here's the bottom line: I've given you many examples of how to close. They're tools. So don't give up. Keep going back.

A friend of mine, Dick Timbers, worked in the printing business for 19 years. In all that time he had been unable to sell anything to one particular company. Finally, he started his own company in a totally different business. At that point, he went back to this customer and said, "Look, for 19 years I've never sold you. I'm never going to see you again in this business." He got an order for $50,000.

So keep going back. In every seminar I ask, "How many of you, when you first met your husband or wife, or your current boy friend or girl friend, thought he or she was a jerk?" It's a funny thing: I've never seen a guy raise his hand, but about 30% of the women do! Somebody had to keep trying, to keep going back.

Point 18. From the buyer's side.

The buyer answers nine specific questions, either consciously or subconsciously, in arriving at the decision to buy. You do this every time you make a purchase.

The questions:

1. Why should I see you?
2. Why should I listen to you?
3. What is my problem?
4. How are you going to solve it?
5. Why should I trust you?
6. Why should I trust my company to your company?
7. Why is your solution best?
8. Why should I take action?
9. Why should I buy now?

These questions go through your mind when you're buying. Do the same questions go through your customer's mind? Absolutely.

Point 19. Getting through the valleys.

Salespersons go through a peak-and-valley syndrome. When a salesperson has a good month, sales usually drop the next month because the salesperson went on a mental vacation.

I often see salespeople get into a valley and then stay there a while. They have a bad month, and they start getting bummed out. They get depressed and beat themselves up. Then they think about quitting.

Instead they need to do what any good doctor does: diagnose the problem and fix it. To fix it, you have to find out what you've been doing wrong, and you have to find new business. Most people don't fix the problem, but you want to be sure *you* do. So I give you a 25-point checklist:

1. Was I on time for the appointment?
2. Did I establish a need or desire for my product

or service?

3. How was my opening statement received?
4. Did I ask good questions?
5. Did I receive the answers I wanted?
6. How did I appear to the prospect?
7. Did I prejudge the situation?
8. Did I control the interview?
9. Did I speak and act as an equal, or did I assume a superior or subservient attitude?
10. Did I wait for and listen to the prospect's reaction, or did I anticipate his answer and tell him?
11. Did I rush through the presentation to get elsewhere?
12. Was I totally prepared for the presentation, or did I fumble and search?
13. Did I break the prospect's train of thought with an irrelevant statement?
14. Did I try to make the prospect obligated to me?
15. Did I really get to the main objection?
16. How did I prepare the prospect for the final price?
17. Did I treat pricing consistently and persistently?
18. Did I use five or more closes? When?
19. Did I strive to show pride of ownership?
20. What options or alternatives did I give?
21. Did I summarize all the benefits?
22. Did I show how the prospect could profit?
23. Did I show where and how the prospect could profit?
24. Did I show the prospect how others have profited?
25. How do I now feel toward the prospect?

I want to emphasize the final point on this list:

How do I feel toward the prospect?

Usually, the client will feel the way you do: if you like the client, the client will like you; if you don't like the client, the client won't like you. Absolutely. Don't you like most people who buy from you?

Point 20. Why salespeople fail.

A sales trainer named David Sandler has come to the conclusion that salespeople fail because, according to him, 95% of all salespeople are doing it all wrong. He has written a great article on the subject in which he rejects the four generally accepted assumptions about selling.

Assumption #1:

Salespeople should be extroverted. Sandler says *no*. He says:

The better and more experienced the salesperson is, the more he or she knows how to keep a low profile.

Think about this in terms of dating. I ask women in my seminars, "Did you ever meet a guy and all he talks about is how much money he makes? Does it really impress you?" The answer is NO. If the guy has money and doesn't talk about it, but instead just shows confidence, women can tell. Similarly, you don't have to be extroverted to be a good salesperson. You can be enthusiastic. Just keep in mind that it's your job to be the cardiologist of sales.

Assumption #2:

The salesperson must learn everything about the product.

Sandler says *no*, that most salespeople want to describe product benefits before the prospect is interested. They want to impress the prospect with how much they know. They aren't focused on the buyer.

Sandler's motto is:

Sell today, educate tomorrow.

Personally, I would modify this to:

Sell today, educate the customer today on what he or she wants to know.

I'm sure that a lot of things you sell in connection with your product or service are not important to your customer today. So why go through them now? You'll probably just confuse the customer if you try to sell them everything upfront. Go slowly. Take one step at a time.

Assumption #3:

Always ask for the order and be prepared for objections.

Sandler says *no*. Instead:

Never ask for the order. Always bring up objections before the customer thinks of them.

Personally, I have a little problem with that. I believe you should always ask for the order. I wouldn't go out of my way to bring up objections the customer might never think of. Of course, I deal with objections when I do hear them. Let me tell you a story about Ford.

When I owned Direct Opinions, I had a national contract with all Ford dealers to monitor customer service. Once a year, at a meeting of Ford dealers, we presented the questions my employees asked of all Ford customers. And every year I got objections from these dealers. They'd say things like, "How do you know your employees actually call our customers?" or, "We think your employees make up these answers." Or, "Your employees must make these calls at the wrong time," or "These comments are worthless because your employees aren't trained properly."

So I made a list of these dealers' top ten objections and my responses, and I overcame every objection. Guess what. Those objections stopped.

So if you have objections that your customers might have, bring them up. Be sure that you can answer them. You come across as a more honest person. Also, if you can anticipate an objection and answer it well, it is no longer an objection.

Assumption #4:

The super salesperson is a great talker.

Sandler says *no*. Instead:

The super salesperson is a great listener.

Sandler tells how he handles unfriendly prospects:

Prospect: "I'm not interested."

Sandler: "Maybe you shouldn't be. Let me ask you a question. What is it that you're not interested in?"

Prospect: "I don't want to spend the money."

Sandler: "Let me ask you a question. How much were you planning on spending?"

And so on…it's all a matter of asking questions.

That's what selling is all about:

Selling is asking, not telling.

Selling is listening, not talking.

If you take just one thing away from this book, take those two sentences. Memorize them. Make them part of your life.

Selling is asking, not telling.

Selling is listening, not talking.

If you do that, you will be unbelievable in sales and in your personal life, because you will know how to communicate with people.

Whether the relationships are with your boss or your employees, your customers or your prospects, your family or your significant other, it's all the same.

Finally, if I can leave you with just one thought, it's this:

Make selling fun. Give it your best and most enthusiastic effort every day. If you do that, you can be the best. If I can do it, *you* can do it!

About the Author

In 1977, at the age of 22, Hal Becker became the Xerox Corporation's top salesperson in a sales force of 11,000 people throughout the United States.

In 1982 Hal founded Direct Opinions in order to help companies in various industries to achieve customer satisfaction through telemarketing. The company grew to offices throughout the United States and Canada conducting two million calls annually. One example might be the phone call you received after taking your car in for service at your new-car dealership, asking if you were satisfied with the work performed.

Hal Becker has taken his techniques and applied them, not only to building his own organization, but also to helping thousands of others learn how to be the best.

In 1990 he sold Direct Opinions so he could dedicate more time to the many lectures and seminars he conducts around the country. His seminars, geared to both experienced and inexperienced salespersons, incorporate serious selling methods with pure fun.

Hal's personal experience with terminal cancer at age 28 led to the founding of the Cancer Hotline, a telephone service that provides support and information for cancer patients and their families.

For additional copies of this book, or to arrange for Hal Becker to present a speech or seminar, contact:

The Becker Group
6785 Ridgecliff Drive
Solon, Ohio 44139

Phone: (440) 542-9884
FAX: (440) 542-9886
Internet: www.halbecker.com